INTERNATIONAL ENCYCLOPEDIA OF ART

North American Art to 1900

first edition

Arleen Pancza-Graham

Facts On File, Inc.

INTERNATIONAL ENCYCLOPEDIA OF ART
NORTH AMERICAN ART TO 1900

*Cataloging-in-Publication Data
available on request from Facts On File, Inc.*

Facts on File books are available at special discounts when purchased in bulk quantities
for businesses, associations, institutions or sales promotions. Please call our Special
Sales Department in New York at 212/967-8800 or 800/322-8755.

This is a Mirabel Book produced by:
Cynthia Parzych Publishing Inc.
648 Broadway
New York, NY 10012

For Caroline and the next generation of American art historians.

Edited by: Frances Helby
Designed by: Dorchester Typesetting Group Ltd.
Printed and bound in Spain by: Imschoot Graphic Service

Front cover: The portrait of *Mrs. Elizabeth Freake and Baby Mary* was painted about
1674 by an anonymous limner.

10 9 8 7 6 5 4 3 2 1

Contents

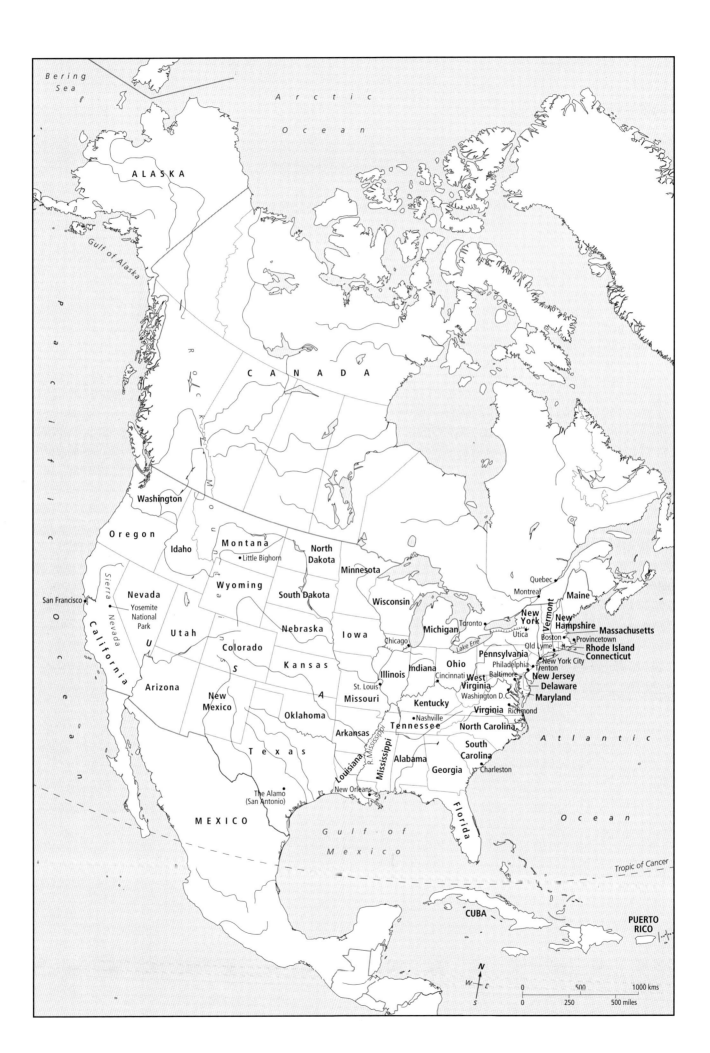

Introduction

The history of art in North America, and more particularly the United States, tells the story of the development of a new nation seen through the language of vision. It is a nation of many different people, religions, political beliefs and economic backgrounds. At first, it was a country that valued art for practical purposes—to record how the land looked or a person appeared. As America became more securely established, so too did the visual arts. To understand the history of the visual arts in America, we must study the visual vocabulary that artists use.

The American Indians, North America's first artists, used signs and symbols on the exterior of tepees or the patterns that decorated their costumes to identify the social status of a person or tribe. European artists who saw an opportunity for a more prosperous career in colonial America came to record not only the images of a new country but also to fill the demand for portraits. As time passed, the colonists themselves began to try to imitate the work of European-trained artists, for America lacked the art academies and teachers found in Europe and fine examples of the work of past masters to study and copy. Shortly before the American Revolution in 1776, Americans who were seriously interested in art, like the Pennsylvania-born artist Benjamin West (1738–1820), began to travel abroad. Some, like West, never returned, and began the story of the expatriate American artist. Others improved their craft and returned home, better able to produce the professional portraits that were in great demand.

By 1782, art had become so important to Americans that the artist and entrepreneur Charles Willson Peale (1741–1827) opened his Gallery of Famous Men in Philadelphia, that he expanded four years later to a museum that also covered natural history. That year also saw the publication of the first magazine to include

Timeline

This timeline lists some of the important events, both historical (listed above the time bar) and art historical (below) that have been mentioned in this book. While every event cannot be mentioned it is hoped that this diagram will help the reader to understand at a glance how these events relate in time.

1492: Christopher Columbus lands in the Bahamas and Cuba and founds the first new world settlements.

from 1492: American Indians come into contact with Europeans. Some travel to Europe. As their land is gradually taken, different American Indian groups are forced into greater contact with each other.

1700s: Colonization by Europeans increases, communities grow and people begin to feel settled in the new world. Unrest increases in the American colonies over the lack of political control and "taxation without representation."

20,000–8,000 B.C.: The first human beings wander into the Americas during the last Ice Age.

20,000 B.C.–1200 A.D.

1492–1600s A.D.

1700–1750 A.D.

From 20,000: Indians in America make rock carvings and paintings, masks, totem poles and stone carvings.

about 1000 B.C.–1200 A.D.: The Inuit carve ivory and bone figures, decorate utilitarian objects with line engravings and make masks for dancers and healers.

by the late 1500s: European artists, who often had a religious mission, record the appearance of Indians and the flora and fauna of the new world.

by the 1600s: Anonymous, untrained limners paint portraits of settlers and Indians for American settlers.

1663: The first European artist settles in Quebec.

1715–1730 A.D.: The first American school of painting, the Patroon Painters, emerges.

1728: John Smibert becomes the first professionally trained artist to come to America. He holds the first art exhibition in America at his Boston Art Studio.

mid-1700s: The first professional, female sculptor Patience Lovell Wright makes portrait busts in wax.

engravings as illustrations, the *Columbian*. In 1805, the Pennsylvania Academy of Fine Arts was founded and in 1826, the National Academy of Design was organized in New York. They are still in existence.

Successful business people such as the New Yorker, Luman Reed (1785–1836), bought works by American artists. Reed's collection, like others after his, eventually became the foundation of a major public institution, the New-York Historical Society. By 1834, it was even possible for William Dunlap (1766–1839) to write the first *History of American Art*.

As the number of artists increased, so too did the kinds of paintings that were created. Portrait painting was the most popular. Landscape paintings not only gave an idea of the natural majesty and beauty of this new country, but also suggested its potential political power. Along with paintings of American historical events, they made an important contribution to the national image.

The folk art tradition, much like a local dialect, served the continuing, practical needs of an emerging nation. It often reflected the lives of a broad cross section of Americans. Genre paintings depicting everyday scenes became popular and celebrated American life.

As more and more art was exhibited, it quite naturally became a subject to write about. "Puffery pieces" designed to publicize artists' recent works and exhibitions later gave way to more considered critical essays. In 1855, the first really professional art magazine in America, *The Crayon* was published. Ten years later, writers such as James Jackson Jarves (1818–88) in his book *The Art-Idea* and Clarence Cook (1828–1900), writing in *The New Path*, expressed their authoritarian ideas about how an artist could create "good" art. These writers stressed direct observation of nature. Women writers such as Marianna Griswold van Rensselaer (1851–1934) or the Paris-based writer Lucy Hooper (1835–93) also contributed much to art criticism in the nineteenth century.

As the Civil War divided the nation, it also disrupted the American art scene. Photography, which recorded the horror of the war, slowly became a new means of artistic expression. Initially it was used by American artists to help them remember and work out their compositions.

Artists went abroad in increasing numbers to study in

1776: The Declaration of Independence is made and the U.S.A. is formed. War with Great Britain continues until 1783 when Great Britain recognizes the new country's independence. Foreign recognition of the U.S. increases. The remaining British–controlled area in North America becomes the colony of Canada.

1784–89: Thomas Jefferson, the author of the Declaration of Independence, becomes American Minister in Paris.

1776–1800 A.D.

1760s: American artists begin to travel particularly to London and paint abroad.

from 1765: Paul Revere makes political prints documenting events leading up to independence.

1770/71: American history painting begins with *The Death of General Wolfe* by Benjamin West.

1782: America's first museum opens in Philadelphia.

1784–89: Thomas Jefferson comes into contact with European art and Palladian architecture. He brings their influence to the U.S.

---

from about 1800: America is full of progress and inventions.

1803: The Louisiana Territory is purchased by the U.S. and the West is opened.

1812: The Oregon Trail is opened.

1800–approx 1820 A.D.

early 1800s: The Neo-Classical style predominates in America, where it is called the Federal style. It becomes the national style for public buildings and great houses. Romanticism appears in painting. The Hudson River school of allegorical landscape painting emerges.

about 1800: The first professional sculptor William Rush works in wood.

1805: The Pennsylvania Academy of Fine Arts is founded.

1817: Eight history murals are commissioned for the U.S. Capitol.

1840s: Large numbers of people follow the Oregon Trail West and in 1842 it is mapped.

1848: Texas joins the U.S., first women's rights convention is held in Seneca Falls, New York and gold is discovered in California.

by the 1850s: Railways are built and industrialization begins in the U.S.

1839–1850s A.D.

1826: The National Academy of Design is founded.

1827: John James Audubon publishes *Birds of North America*.

1839–52: The American Art-Union promotes painting and prints of American life and leads to the rise of genre painting.

mid-1800s: Touring art exhibitions appear.

the ateliers or studios of Europe. At first, many of them went to Germany to study in Dusseldorf and Munich. Gradually, Paris replaced these cities and became a center for American art students. During the last quarter of the nineteenth century, the French style of painting known as Impressionism influenced many of the American painters who went to France, as well as the increasing number of wealthy American collectors. Two important world's fairs were held in America. The Centennial Exposition of 1876 and the World's Columbian Exposition of 1893 displayed art both by American artists and in American collections.

By 1900, the visual arts in America were no longer based solely on practical concerns and western European models. Japanese art, for example, became an important influence on American painters. The support system for the professional artist was also firmly in place. Connoisseurs like William T. Evans (1843–1918) and Thomas B. Clarke (1849–1931) began to acquire collections of American art. The Art Students League in New York was one of many art schools that had been founded. Artists attracted to picturesque locales such as Provincetown, Massachusetts; Old Lyme, Connecticut and East Hampton, New York, formed summer colonies. During the rest of the year, artists gathered together in numerous clubs and organizations established in cities throughout the country. Art publications and exhibition reviews were published regularly. Great museums such as the Metropolitan Museum in New York and the Museum of Fine Arts, Boston, along with commercial galleries and auction houses had all been established. International exhibitions such as one held in Paris in 1889 gave American artists the opportunity to exhibit their art to a world audience. Regional exhibitions exposed citizens throughout the country to American and foreign art. Photography gave artists new opportunities for visual expression.

By the close of the nineteenth century, it was possible to speak of a history of American art and to see the history of this new nation unfold visually, by looking at works of art that were truly American. Artists, now fluent in their use of line, color, texture, shape and space, used these basic visual elements to relate the American experience. By observing how they used this basic visual vocabulary, we too can look at the past and see how the story of North America's visual heritage unfolds.

---

mid–1800s: Increasing industrialization in the North leads to a divide with the agricultural, slave-supported South. The issues of slavery and abolition lead to the Civil War.

1861–65: The Civil War.

mid-1800s–1864 A.D.

late 1830s: Photography is brought to America.

in the mid-1800s: Americans, including women, travel to Italy and begin to learn to make sculptures in marble.

from about 1850: Prints of American life are widely available.

1861–65: Artists record the Civil War. Photographers take harrowing pictures of the war of a kind never seen before.

1864–76: There is a period of Reconstruction for the damaged and divided U.S. It leads to a time of prosperity for some called the Gilded Age.

1876: The Centennial Exposition is held in Philadelphia. It reflects America's increasing industrialization, urbanization, confidence and openness to foreign ideas.

1864–1876 A.D.

1865–76: Artists take inspiration from the Civil War, the issues of freedom and slavery, and the problems of reuniting and rebuilding a partly destroyed and divided society.

1860s–70s: Realism is used to portray the life of the working classes.

1870s: Increasing numbers of artists leave to study abroad.

late 1800s: The U.S. experiences a time of confidence and affluence.

1873: Mark Twain's The Gilded Age is published.

from 1883: Increasing waves of immigrants come to the U.S. and are not always welcome.

1886: The American Federation of Labor is founded.

1893: The World's Columbian Exposition in Chicago commemorates the 400th anniversary of Columbus's discovery of the Americas and displays America's position in the world.

1876–1900 A.D.

1876: Regional art exhibitions take place and circulating exhibitions take art around the country. Artists paint in the open air and artists' colonies emerge.

1886: Americans are introduced to French Impressionism at a New York exhibition.

1893: The World's Columbian Exposition is "the greatest meeting of artists since the fifteenth century!"

1 Images of the North American Indian

A Winnebago Poem__

American Indians have always had strong feeling and respect for nature. From the earliest images on rocks to poetry, their artistic heritage exhibits a sensitivity to their environment. This Winnebago poem entitled "This Newly Created World" may be very ancient. It was probably handed down by oral tradition and translated in the nineteenth century.

> *Pleasant it looked,*
> *this newly created world.*
> *Along the entire length and breadth*
> *of the earth, our grandmother,*
> *extended the green reflection*
> *of her covering*
> *and the escaping odors*
> *were pleasant to inhale.* ■

▲ *This ancient wall painting is typical of the earliest forms of art produced by American Indian tribes in the southwest United States.*

The history of the visual arts in North America began long before European settlers arrived on the continent. Although their art is not as widely known as that of the prehistoric people of Europe, the first American Indians also recorded the world around them on canyon walls and in stone caves. This prehistoric rock art may take two forms: petroglyphs, or carved images, and pictographs or paintings on rock. Through them, these early inhabitants were able to tell us much about their beliefs and the world around them. Images of the weapons they used, the gods they worshipped and the animals they hunted are all preserved in these stone works. Some of these images have survived more than 11,000 years. They were first noticed by early English settlers in Massachusetts, and later by Father Jacques Marquette (1637–75), the French missionary who explored the Mississippi River in 1673. However, it was not until the late nineteenth century that a scientific study of rock art was made.

In addition to their rock art, the American Indians also contributed to the visual arts in North America through the material objects they

▲ *Wood carvings such as these totem poles sometimes helped to ensure the success of a hunt or identify a family.*

Potlatch Parties_____

The most important social occasion for members of Canada's Tlingit, Haida, Kwakiutl, Salish and Makah tribes living on the northwest coast of North America was the *potlatch* feast. Many different carved objects such as totem poles, spoons and bowls were made for use at the ceremonies at these feasts held to mark important occasions such as the naming of children, marriages or deaths. The word *potlatch* means "to give" in the Chinook language. Guests were given gifts for attending. ■

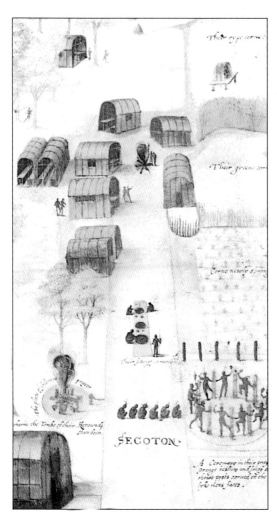

▲ *John White was one of the first Europeans to create images of the native American Indians and their culture. This watercolor of the Indian village of Secoton was painted after 1585.*

Subarctic Art _____

The Inuit people who live in the area extending from the Aleutian Islands and Alaska through Canada to Greenland have one of the oldest cultures in North America. Their ancient art forms, created from about 1000 B.C. to 1200 A.D., include carved figures in ivory or bone and line engravings cut into utilitarian objects. They also made masks for their hunting festivals, winter ceremonies and for Inuit doctors who wore them to ask a healing spirit for help. ■

Southwest Art Forms _____

The Pueblo Indians of New Mexico and Arizona practiced the art of pottery-making for centuries. The decorations on their bowls, jars and dishes date far back into history. The Pueblos believe that their souls come from and return to a place called the *kiva* inhabited by spirits called *kachinas*. Pueblo children learn about *kachinas* through small, costumed sculptures that represent these spirits. Special rituals call the *kachinas* from the other world and included the creation of sacred sand paintings. Navajo medicine men developed their sand paintings into an art form. Since the sand paintings must be destroyed during Navajo ceremonies, their appearance is known only from drawings made by the medicine men or by spectators. ■

created for their daily life and spiritual rituals. Many of them, like masks, totem poles and argillite stone carvings, have pleasing aesthetic qualities as well. They confirm that there was a strong sculptural tradition among these people, particularly among the inhabitants of the northwest coast. However, a painting tradition also existed among these peoples. Abstract designs and geometric patterns decorate the pottery made by the southwestern Indians while symbols and myths are the subject matter of many Pueblo Indian mural paintings. Sometimes these wall paintings reflect scenes from traditional ceremonial life. Although each Indian cultural area may have created different, sometimes unique types of visual expression, there was also interaction between various tribes. As European settlement pushed the native inhabitants from their homeland, interaction between these different cultural areas increased.

Shortly after Christopher Columbus (1451–1506) arrived in the New World in 1492, images of the inhabitants of the Americas themselves began to appear in Europe. In 1513, Gonzalo Fernández de Oviedo y Valdés (1478–1557), an overseer for mines in the West Indies, began his *Historia General y Natural de las Indias*. When it was published in Spain in 1535, it contained the first known illustrations of native culture. The appearance and way of life of the Indians who lived in the areas that are now the states of Virginia and Florida was first recorded by an English artist, John White (1543–93). Many of these paintings can now be found in the British Museum. These watercolors, along with other paintings by Jacques Le Moyne, later became the basis for engravings by Theodor de Bry (1529–98), a Flemish goldsmith. In 1590, they appeared in *America*, a multivolume work on the new world published by de Bry.

European settlement of the North American continent eventually

9

▲ *Pocahontas was painted in oil on canvas as she appeared in 1616 after her marriage.*

An American Indian Princess

Pocahontas, the daughter of the Indian chief Powhatan, married the English colonist John Rolfe who first went to Virginia in 1610. Rolfe is thought to be the first person to cultivate tobacco in America. After her marriage, Pocahontas, left America for England, where she was known as Rebecca Rolfe. She died there in 1617, a year after her arrival, just as she was about to return to America. John Rolfe returned to Virginia after her death and became a member of the First Council of State. ■

caused the native inhabitants of the land to be placed in contact with artists who wanted to record their images for posterity. An anonymous artist painted a portrait of the American Indian princess, Pocahontas (1595–1617), about 1616 as she appeared after her marriage to the Englishman, John Rolfe (1585–1622), when she was known as Rebecca. About one hundred years later, another anonymous painter decorated the stairwell of a house in New Hampshire with full length portraits of Indian chieftains dressed in their native regalia. One of these is illustrated below on the left. In 1730, a delegation of Cherokee chiefs visited London to sign a friendship treaty with King George II (1683–1760). The printing technique of engraving allowed many copies of this image to be made so the appearance of these American Indian visitors could be made known to the curious.

The United States of America began to grow and so, too, did the

▲ *Early images of the American Indian includes this regal 1716 portrait.*

▲ *George Catlin produced hundreds of scenes of American Indian life including* The Last Race, Part of Okipa Ceremony *of 1832.*

▲ *Sitting Bull (left) was photographed about 1885 with "Buffalo Bill" Cody, a white man he respected.*

In Rescue *by Horatio Greenough, carved in marble 1837–53, the figure of the American Indian is stopped from an attack on the settlers (at left). The statue, commissioned by Congress, stood on the steps of the Capitol until 1958 when it was removed because it embarrassed some and upset others.*▼

American Indian Martyrs

Among the many American Indians who died for their people, two names stand out for their bravery. Crazy Horse (approx. 1849–77) and Sitting Bull (approx. 1834–90) were both Sioux leaders. In 1876, they joined forces to resist the efforts of the U.S. government to take their lands and confine their people to reservations. Both contributed to the defeat of General George Armstrong Custer (1839–76) at the Battle of Little Big Horn in June of 1876. Crazy Horse surrendered to the U.S. Army the following year voluntarily but he was killed in the scuffle to force him into a jail cell. Sitting Bull was given amnesty and settled on a reservation. He toured with Buffalo Bill's Wild West Show. However, he too was later shot by captors and died on December 15, 1890. ■

importance of making a visual record of the native people. In 1821, the American artist, Charles Bird King (1785–1862) was hired by the United States government to paint the portraits of important Indians when they visited Washington D.C. Another artist who devoted much of his career to painting the appearance and activities of the Indians and the landscapes inhabited by them, was George Catlin (1796–1872). Beginning in 1830, he spent eight years traveling among various tribes, carefully recording their lifestyles. After completing his *Indian Gallery*, which included 507 paintings, he took the paintings, along with a group of Indians to England and France.

As the American Indians' situation changed over time, so too did the way they were represented in the visual arts. Initially, the main interest in painting and sculpture was simply to record exotic images of these unknown natives but the role of the American Indian in American art changed. Occasionally included as an observer of the activities of the new European settlers by artists such as Benjamin West (1738–1820), the Indians were later depicted as a threat to the settlers. Their attempts to preserve their ancestral land despite the many injustices forced upon them, were usually perceived as hostile acts that required military action.

In time, the American Indian became the romantic symbol of a strong new nation. Sculptors like Augustus Saint-Gaudens (1848–1907) used mythical Indians as models for statues of poetic characters such as Henry Wadsworth Longfellow's (1807–82), Hiawatha. As the nineteenth century drew to a close other artists like the sculptor Solon Hannibal Borglum (1868–1922) summed up the sad situation of the noble American Indian in subdued images of these native people.

2 The Portrait in Colonial America

John Singleton Copley (1738–1815), who painted in the colonies in the years before the Revolutionary War, is often thought of as America's first great artist because of the many fine portraits that he painted. In a letter to a friend, he wrote about how important portraits were in the new nation. He said that: "Was it not for preserving the resemblance of particular persons, painting would not be known in the place." Portraits of all types were created in order to record the image of an individual for future generations.

Many of the earliest portraits were made by traveling artists called limners who also painted or illuminated signs for local shops and businesses. The names of many of these painters, like the one who depicted *Mrs. Elizabeth Freake and Baby Mary* are unknown. Since there were no art schools, most of these early American artists were self-taught and their talents were limited. As they journeyed along the eastern seaboard, these folk artists captured basic likenesses of many members of the early colonial families, particularly from New England to New York.

About six of these itinerant painters worked in the area of the Hudson River Valley of New York between 1715 and 1730. They are called the Patroon Painters after the wealthy Dutch settlers who commissioned pictures from them. Although the actual identities of the painters are not all known with certainty, their styles are similar. Together they form the first school of painting in the American colonies.

Some artists who began their careers by studying art in their native lands realized that there was less competition in America. A few went to the colonies where their talents were

▲ *The anonymous limner, probably untrained, who painted* Mrs. Elizabeth Freake and Baby Mary *in oil about 1674, had a good sense of line and pattern.*

Jesuit Artists in Canada

Western Art was introduced into Canada by the Jesuits, who explored North America. Portraits of members of religious communities have been attributed to Abbé Hugues Pommier (1637–86) who arrived in Quebec in 1664 and taught there for five years. Père Louis Nicolas (1634–approx. 1701) produced a collection of eighty-one watercolors and pen and ink drawings of flowers, animals and natives of the new world. A third Jesuit in Canada, Père Claude Chauchetière (1645–1709), used his art to spread his faith. He was assigned to the Iroquois mission in 1678 and made drawings to illustrate his teachings. ■

John Smibert was born in Scotland and ▶
although well trained and known, he was not a
major painter. He came to America with many
copies of European paintings. His Boston
studio was a gathering place for many of
America's early artists. He painted this 1729 oil
on canvas entitled The Bermuda Group.

Limning a Likeness ___

Before the American Revolution, painting was usually called limning. It was a
word that came from the old English tradition of manuscript illumination. Limning is a word that sounds much like the
way the work could be described—a line
painting that depicted someone's likeness, without many shadows. This helped
to define the subject clearly and preserve a person's image. Not only was this
something that the prosperous colonists
wanted but it also gave the paintings a
very decorative quality. Many of these
limners were self-taught. They often did
more than "take a likeness." They also
painted signs, frames and sold art supplies to make a living as they traveled
from place to place. ■

▲ *Many Americans visiting England in the*
1770s met the celebrated artist Patience Lovell
Wright, including President John Adams's wife
Abigail. The artist is shown with one of her
wax works in this 1775 engraving from The
London Magazine.

welcomed. John Smibert (1688–1751) was one such artist.
Considered to be the first fully trained professional artist to come to
the American colonies, Smibert arrived in 1728. He had hoped to
serve as a painting instructor at a college to be founded by the Anglo-
Irish philosopher Bishop Berkeley (1685–1753), whom he painted
along with his entourage in the 1729 painting known as *The
Bermuda Group*. The college was never established and Smibert
settled in Boston where his art studio presented the earliest art
exhibitions held in America. He also opened the first shop for art
supplies in the colonies. During his career, he painted over 225
portraits. They gave American artists, who usually copied European
prints, a direct example of how to paint in a professional style.

America's first portraits in pastels were produced by another
newcomer to America—a woman. Henrietta Deering Johnston (before
1670–approx. 1728), the wife of a clergyman and originally from
Dublin, Ireland, arrived in South Carolina in 1708. She produced
over forty pastel drawings of local notables and her husband said,
"Were it not for the assistance my wife gives me by drawing of
pictures...I shou'd not have been able to live."

Another woman who made an early mark in both American
portraiture and women's history was Patience Lovell Wright
(1725–86), a Quaker from Bordentown, New Jersey. She is
considered America's first professional woman sculptor. After her
husband's death, she supported her family by creating portrait busts
in wax. She and her sister also developed a successful waxworks show
and, in 1772, she sailed for England to continue her career. Despite
the fact that she was an outspoken supporter of American
independence and civil liberties, she was invited to create a wax
portrait of King George III (1738–1820).

◀ *This is the engraved portrait of the poet Phillis Wheatley that appeared with an English edition of her poems published in 1773.*

A Poet's Portrait

In America, before the War of Independence, most colonial era portraits were of distinguished white citizens. African-Americans usually appeared only as incidental or background figures serving their white masters. However there were a few exceptions. Portraits like that of the African-American poet, Phillis Wheatley (approx. 1753–85), served to record the author's likeness for an edition of her poetry. Wheatley was unusual for her day. She was an educated black woman who worked as a domestic for a Boston family. In her free time she wrote poetry. This is an extract from her poem "Liberty and Peace:"

> Lo! Freedom comes. Th' prescient
>   Muse foretold,
> All Eyes th' accomplish'd Prophecy
>   behold:
> Her Port describ'd, "She moves
>   divinely fair,
> Olive and Laurel bind her golden
>   Hair." ∎

▲ *Paul Revere is usually remembered as a patriot, however, he was a craftsman by training and made many beautiful silver objects. In John Singleton Copley's oil on canvas of 1768–70, Revere is shown at work, with engraving tools at his side as he thinks about a design for his undecorated teapot. It is one of only a few portraits of colonial crafts people.*

John Singleton Copley painted over 350 American portraits. Many were of colonial society figures and included costumes, furniture and settings that suggested that the sitter was a wealthy individual. However, none was more famous than that of the patriot, Paul Revere (1735–1818). At the onset of the War of Independence, Copley chose to leave America and settle in London with his family where he continued to paint portraits.

Copley was not the first American to leave the colonies for

◀ *People like Paul Revere who worked in metal often also produced engravings. Their talent for working with the hard material was also useful for making prints. He made this engraving of* The Bloody Massacre at Boston, March 5, 1770, *after a drawing by Henry Pelham.*

▲ *The well-known inventor, Robert Fulton, was an engineer, but went to London in 1786 to study art before deciding on a career. This marble statue of him was made in 1883 by Howard Roberts (1843–1900).*

◄ *This self-portrait was painted by Benjamin West's student Matthew Pratt in oil on canvas in 1764.*

William Penn, the Quaker who settled ► *Pennsylvania, negotiated a peace treaty with the Lenni-Lenape Indians in the Delaware Valley area in 1682. Benjamin West painted* William Penn's Treaty with the Indians *in oil on canvas in 1771.*

An Artist and Inventor _____

Today, Robert Fulton (1765–1815) is remembered as the American who invented the steamboat. His ship, the *Clermont*, began a new era in the history of navigation. Few people realize that Fulton began his career as a professional artist. He followed his fellow Pennsylvanian, Benjamin West to London and studied art with him from 1786 to 1793. He specialized in portrait and miniature painting before becoming an inventor. ■

England. Another American artist, Benjamin West, came from Pennsylvania and specialized in history paintings. He arrived in London in 1763 and was the first American artist to achieve international fame. He was also a popular teacher. One of his pupils, Matthew Pratt (1734–1805), paid tribute to him and to some of his other fellow-countrymen in a group portrait of the students in West's London studio called *The American School*.

Another American who knew both Copley and West while living in London was Gilbert Stuart (1755–1828). Born in Rhode Island, Stuart moved to England in 1775 during its golden age of portrait painting and quickly absorbed the skills of Great Britain's distinguished painters. By the time he returned to America in 1792, he had had a successful career in both London and Dublin. Stuart's elegant manner allowed him to capture a likeness with minimum effort and he quickly became the most popular portrait painter in post-Revolutionary America. He is particularly remembered for his several portraits of the first president, George Washington (1732–99) painted from life.

3   The World of Thomas Jefferson

▲ *Popular portraits were often copied by other artists. Gilbert Stuart's portrait of Thomas Jefferson was copied or replicated by Asher B. Durand thirty-six years after Stuart painted it.*

Democracy Seen Through French Eyes

Alexis de Tocqueville (1805–59) arrived in the U.S. in 1831 and began a ten-month cross-country tour. The young French aristocrat felt this was a country without art, literature or eloquence. He thought people were only interested in money. Yet they also had a genuine concern for liberty and the well-being of their community, unlike his countrymen in France. ■

Thomas Jefferson considered his design for ▶ *the architecture of the University of Virginia at Charlottesville his greatest achievement.*

Thomas Jefferson (1743–1826) is perhaps best remembered as the author of the American Declaration of Independence. However, during his lifetime he had a variety of interests and accomplished many things. As the third president of the United States, from 1801 to 1809, he approved the purchase of the Louisiana Territory from France which doubled the size of the country. He was also an architect and today the buildings he designed are reminders of his achievements in the visual arts.

From 1784 to 1789, Jefferson served as U.S. Minister to France. There he not only witnessed the early stages of the French Revolution, but also came to know many French and British artists and intellectuals. Visits to art exhibitions at the French Salon introduced him to paintings by artists such as Jacques Louis David (1748–1825) and helped him to learn about art. When the Virginia legislature asked Jefferson's advice concerning a proposed statue of George Washington for the Virginia State Capitol, he suggested that the best choice for a sculptor was the Frenchman, Jean Antoine Houdon (1741–1828).

Although Jefferson had some interest in painting and sculpture, it was the architecture he saw abroad that interested him most. It was also the area of the arts in which he made his most important contribution. While still a young man, he received some basic training in architecture, and he continued to design buildings throughout his life. He believed that housing was one of the primary necessities for the growing young republic. While he was U.S. Minister to France, Jefferson saw Roman ruins in Italy and was particularly impressed by the Italian architect, Andrea Palladio (1508–80). Palladio's ideas are

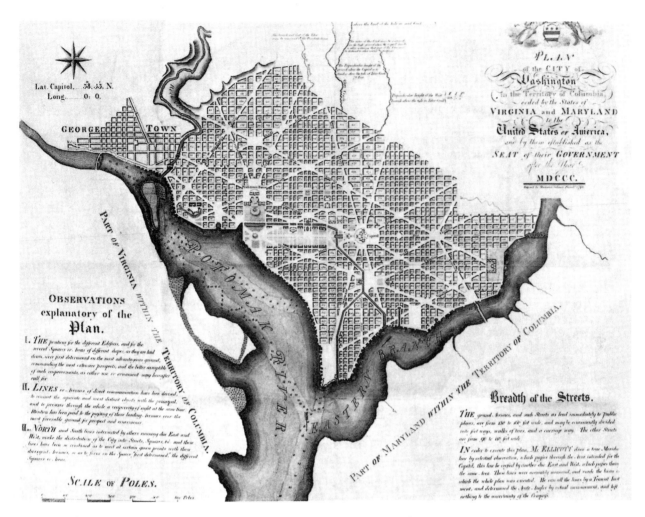

▲ Many of the measurements and calculations for Jefferson's and L'Enfant's plan of Washington D.C. were made by Benjamin Banneker a free black. Jefferson thought him very talented and "a respectable mathematician," a comment Jefferson made in a letter written in 1791.

Sacajawea

One of Thomas Jefferson's important accomplishments as president was the Louisiana Purchase in 1803. He organized an expedition led by his secretary, Meriwether Lewis (1774–1809) and William Clark (1770–1838) to map this vast new territory. One of the guides on the Lewis and Clark Expedition was married to a woman named Sacajawea, who was a member of the Shoshone tribe. She served as interpreter and peacemaker. ■

reflected in Jefferson's own home, Monticello, which he worked on for many years. Besides Palladio, Jefferson was especially influenced by the classical form of a small Roman temple in Nîmes, France, called the *Maison Carrée*. It was the inspiration for Jefferson's design for the state capitol at Richmond, Virginia. It also helped to establish an official national style for the young republic that could be adapted for many government buildings, educational institutions and even housing. Under Jefferson's careful supervision, and the practical planning of the French engineer Major Pierre-Charles L'Enfant (1754–1825), the new seat of government in Washington, D.C. progressed in 1791. However, of all the many architectural projects Jefferson was involved in, he considered the University of Virginia to be his greatest achievement. He called it an "academical village." It was so important to him that he included it in the epitaph he wrote for his tombstone as one of his three great accomplishments.

▲ *Captain Perry is best remembered by his victory statement: "We have met the enemy and they are ours." Rembrandt Peale produced this portrait of Captain Perry.*

The War of 1812 _____

Once again, in 1812 Americans went to war with the British. The American Revolution won independence from Great Britain, but not international respect. The British captured U.S. ships, interfered with trade and armed the American Indians so that settlers in the Northwest Territory were attacked. Captain Oliver H. Perry's (1767–1845) victory at the battle of Lake Erie in September 1813 ended British plans to invade the United States from Canada. When Andrew Jackson defeated the British in New Orleans in January 1815, he became a national hero. Many of the people and events associated with the War of 1812 were celebrated through the arts. ■

The art and architecture of the post-Revolutionary period in which Jefferson lived is called Neo-Classical in Europe because it was inspired by the classical past. In America, that same period is named Federal, because during that time, the various states came together to form the federation of the United States of America. Characteristics of the Federal style included large flat surfaces, refined classical details, simple columns and a feeling of restrained elegance that can be found in much of the art and architecture from the period. Sometimes, architects like Benjamin H. Latrobe (1764–1820) added details such as corncobs, tobacco leaves and stars to make buildings uniquely American. Latrobe, who was born and schooled in England, was the first fully trained architect to work in the United States.

Even William Rush (1756–1833), America's first professional sculptor was involved with architecture. He created large figures of *Comedy* and *Tragedy* for the Chestnut Street Theater in Philadelphia, Pennsylvania, in 1808. Later he completed his most famous work, *Water Nymph and Bittern* for the fountain that stood in front of Latrobe's waterworks, also in Philadelphia. Although he worked in wood, Rush was the first American sculptor whose work measured up to European standards.

Philadelphia was also the home of Charles Willson Peale who has already been mentioned. Although active as a portrait painter, Peale, like Jefferson, had many interests. In 1782, he opened the first museum

▲ *Charles Willson Peale (shown at right) painted* Exhuming the First American Mastodon *in 1806–08 in oil on canvas. A man of many interests, he reconstructed the mastodon skeleton from bones he helped dig up. The mastodon became the main exhibition of his collection.*

The Last to Leave

During the War of 1812, the British attacked and burned Washington, D.C. Gilbert Stuart's portrait of George Washington was on view in the White House, and in danger of being destroyed. Rather than risk losing this famous painting, First Lady Dolley Madison (1768–1849) stayed behind to pack up the painting along with important presidential papers and the White House silverware. ■

Beautiful and vivacious, Dolley Madison brought a social glow to the White House, ▶
when her husband took office after the subdued years of Thomas Jefferson's presidency.
This is an anonymous portrait of the popular First Lady.

▲ *Joshua Johnson (active 1796–1824) is considered the earliest professional black artist in America. Born a slave, he was brought to Philadelphia to work. He may have learned about art from a nephew of Charles Willson Peale. Most of his paintings like this one of Daniel Coker, are portraits of people from Baltimore.*

in the country in Philadelphia. Later his family, many of whom were artists themselves, opened another museum in Baltimore that showed not only works of art, but also examples of natural history. His painting, *Exhuming the First American Mastodon*, shows Peale with the partial skeleton of a mastodon that became the prime attraction of his collecton. Peale also established the first organization for artists, an American Academy of the Fine Arts, called the Columbianum in 1794. He was one of two artists to serve on the first board of the Pennsylvania Academy of the Fine Arts, which was founded in 1805.

The Baltimore branch of the Peale family probably helped train America's first professional black artist, Joshua Johnson who was active as a painter from 1796 to 1824. During his career, he painted many decorative portraits of Baltimore's leading families. The African-American subject of one of his paintings, from about 1810, was, like himself, a free black who has been identified as Daniel Coker (1780–1846), a prominent citizen of Baltimore.

New York too had an active community of artists. They formed an organization for drawing classes and exhibitions. By 1826, the year of Jefferson's death, the National Academy of Design was established and, like the Pennsylvania Academy of Fine Arts, continues in operation today. With the founding of the academies and the establishment of other activities for support, art in America gained an ever increasing audience.

An Early African-American Leader

Born a slave in Delaware, the Reverend Absalom Jones (1746–1818) led a group that persuaded the U.S. government to end the African slave trade in 1808. He founded the Free African Society in Philadelphia. When the country was threatened by the British during the War of 1812, he recruited 2,500 free African-Americans to help defend the City of Brotherly Love. ■

4 Romanticism in American Art

▲ *The legends and characters of New York's Hudson River Valley provided the inspiration for Washington Irving's imaginary tale and for John Quidor's 1829 oil on canvas*, The Return of Rip Van Winkle.

Drawing on his memory of Italy's Alban Hills near the Tiber River, Washington Allston painted this haunting Moonlit Landscape. *The artist gives no clue about who the figures are in the foreground, where they are going or why they are included in the painting at all.* ▼

Romanticism is a poetic style of painting usually associated with the early nineteenth century. It often stirs the emotions and deals with imaginary characters from literature or faraway places and events. Sometimes, romantic works of art have a patriotic theme or deal with ideas. American artists of the early nineteenth century began to deal with romantic themes in paintings like John Quidor's (1801–81) *The Return of Rip Van Winkle*. It was based on Washington Irving's (1783–1859) imaginary tale from the days of the Dutch in New York. Throughout the nineteenth century, the work of visionary artists like William Rimmer (1816–79), and Elihu Vedder (1836–1923) serve as visual counterparts to the work of writers

Many of Washington Allston's (1779–1843) paintings were based on stories from the classics and the Old Testament. However, early in his career, he illustrated

Thomas Cole loved the wild beauty of ▶ America and he used this to help him express the theme of the passing of time in his painting The Voyage of Life: Youth *(1849), in oil on canvas. It is part of his famous series.*

An Opera Becomes a Painting

Albert Pinkham Ryder, who was born in the whaling port of New Bedford, Massachusetts, drew on a legend of the sea for his romantic painting, *The Flying Dutchman*, painted in about 1887. A Dutch sea captain is condemned by the devil to sail the ocean until he finds a woman who will love him faithfully. However he is only allowed to go ashore once every seven years. This tale of man against nature was made famous in an opera by the German composer, Richard Wagner (1813–83). ■

Because the artist experimented with his materials and technique, many of Albert Pinkham Ryder's late nineteenth century paintings have cracked and darkened over the years. These effects help to give a mysterious quality to this 1887 oil on canvas scene from the German legend of the Flying Dutchman, doomed to wander the seas forever. ▼

two scenes from Washington Irving's *Knickerbocker's History of New York*. Paintings like his *Moonlit Landscape* invite the viewer to enter a world created by the imagination, where the reason for the meeting between the figures remains forever mysterious.

Although Thomas Cole (1801–48) is best remembered as the founder of the Hudson River School of landscape painters, he made romantic paintings too. His series of paintings called *The Course of Empire*, and *The Voyage of Life* are imaginative pictures that represent ideas. His 1827 painting, *The Last of the Mohicans*, creates a scene from James Fenimore Cooper's (1789–1851) novel of the same title. It was a book that created an image of a wilderness inhabited by natives whose intimacy with the land was unlike anything known in Europe.

The work of romantic artists is distinctive because it is so different from other work produced in the nineteenth century. Such is the painting of Elihu Vedder whose childhood travels included a visit to Cuba. There he saw the sea creature he recalled in his imaginative painting, *The Lair of the Sea Serpent*. Vedder moved to Italy about 1867 where he spent the rest of his life creating fantasies that were sometimes based on European legends.

Albert Pinkham Ryder (1847–1917) worked during the last quarter of the nineteenth century, when the bright, French Impressionist style of painting was becoming popular. His dark, brooding work stands apart from Impressionism and is considered romantic because it recalls imaginary scenes and legends of long ago. Since he experimented with painting techniques, his pictures have not held up well to time and are usually cracked, yet their imaginative style makes them a link between the earlier romantic style of painting in the nineteenth century and later twentieth-century abstract style of painting.

5 Frontier Life

Gold in California

In 1848, gold was discovered at Sutter's mill in California and President James Polk announced to Congress that the state might hold untold wealth. Gold fever swept the country. The American author Bret Harte (1836–1902), wrote about the gold rush in his book, *Tales of the Argonauts*, of 1875. In 1851, Currier and Ives issued a print called *The Gold Seekers* about the California prospectors. ∎

In 1867, Henry Tuckerman (1813–71), who wrote the *Book of the Artists*, said the American art that interested Europeans most was art which had tales of frontier life as its subject. These themes were seen as particularly American because they spoke of adventure, progress and the promise of the prairie. The opening of the West can be traced to the Louisiana Purchase in 1803. After the War of 1812, even more Americans moved to the West to begin a new life. Usually paintings concerned with eyewitness accounts of actual events or everyday genre scenes created the most interest.

The mid-western artist, George Caleb Bingham (1811–79) clearly suggested in his painting, *The Concealed Enemy*, that it was the American Indian who represented the greatest threat to the western settler. Bingham was the first important American artist brought up in the West. Many of his scenes show mid-western life on the river. The artist himself was active in politics and in his paintings of rural elections and politicians he suggests that civilization, no matter how provincial, was slowly moving westward.

Other American artists like George Catlin

◀ The Death of Jane McCrea, *painted in oil on canvas in 1804 by John Vanderlyn, was based on an actual incident from the Revolutionary War. Jane McCrea's scalp was taken to the British for a reward. The setting is not the West, but the painting shows the danger settlers might face on the frontier.*

◀ *Images like George Caleb Bingham's 1845 oil on canvas, The Concealed Enemy, suggest that by the mid-1800s the westward movement of civilization was forcing the Indians to become increasingly wary and hostile.*

The Art-Union

From 1839 until 1852, a remarkable organization called the American Art-Union helped to support and encourage images based on life in America. Subscribers to the Art-Union received a print as a membership benefit. With the membership funds, the Art-Union purchased paintings that were exhibited in its galleries. At the end of each year, a lottery awarded one of the paintings to a member. Since the directors preferred paintings of scenes from American life, artists were no longer so dependent on painting portraits to establish their reputations. ∎

Immigrants to the West made their way ▶
across the country by several trails. In the 1840s,
the Oregon Trail was mapped by U.S. Army
Lieutenant John Charles Fremont (1813–90),
who was guided by the trapper, Christopher
"Kit" Carson (1809–68). It was heavily used by
settlers and well known by the time Albert
Bierstadt painted his picture, The Oregon Trail,
in 1869. The wagon train, accompanied by men
on horseback and a herd of cattle and sheep,
moves slowly westward into the path of the
setting sun. Bierstadt painted this after he
traveled to the West on the famous trail.

▲ *Paintings like George Caleb Bingham's 1845*
oil on canvas, Daniel Boone Escorting a Band
of Pioneers into the Western Country, *sum up*
the experience of an early group of white
settlers who immigrated to the American
frontier. Daniel Boone became a famous figure
who symbolized the courage of individuals who
moved West.

(1796–1872) and Charles Bird King (1785–1862) carefully recorded the exotic appearance of the American Indians. Others recorded the adventures of early pioneers such as Daniel Boone (1735–1820).

In the second half of the nineteenth century, the publishers Currier and Ives circulated prints that helped people to imagine what life was like west of the Mississippi River. Surprisingly, many were completely imaginary. They were made by an Englishman, Arthur Fitzwilliam Tait (1819–1905), who never actually visited the frontier.

The Oregon Trail was established as early as 1812 by Robert Stuart (1785–1848). It took about five months to cover the 2,000 miles between Missouri and Oregon. The journey was undertaken by thousands of people in the 1840s and commemorated by Albert Bierstadt's (1830–1902) painting, *The Oregon Trail.*

Although the military suffered some serious defeats at the hands of the Indians, the United States government eventually forced the Indians onto reservations. Images of the American West became less threatening and more romantic to people in the East as the West became settled and its wilderness was tamed.

The Conestoga Wagon _____

Conestoga wagons usually pulled by mules or oxen, were most often used by families moving to the West. Often thirty or more wagons joined together to form wagon trains for safety and followed a guide. These wagons held everything from farming tools to furniture and became mobile homes for the pioneers. They often appear in paintings of the period. ■

◀ *These wagon train pioneers break for a meal on their trip west.*

6 Visions of the American Landscape

Kindred Spirits

William Cullen Bryant, who is depicted in the painting at right with his friend, Thomas Cole, was the editor of the *New York Evening Post* for fifty years. His reputation as a poet was secured by the publication of his book, *Poems*, in 1821. Many of his poems, such as "To a Waterfowl" and "The Death of the Flowers" are based on careful observations of nature. In his farewell to his friend, Cole, entitled "To Cole, the Painter, Departing for Europe" he wrote:

> *Thine eyes shall see the light of distant*
> *   skies;*
> *Yet, COLE! thy heart shall bear to*
> *   Europe's strand*
> *A living image of our own bright land,*
> *Such as upon thy glorious canvas lies.* ■

▲ *The poet, William Cullen Bryant, is shown with his friend, Thomas Cole, in this 1849 painting entitled* Kindred Spirits *by another Hudson River School artist, Asher B. Durand.*

As the landscape painter, Thomas Cole (1801–48), prepared to depart for Europe in 1829, his friend, William Cullen Bryant (1794–1878) wrote a short poem for him. In it he told Cole that he would see many interesting things. Bryant reminded Cole not to forget America, and to keep that "earlier, wilder image bright." Thomas Cole painted many pictures of scenery, or landscapes. His friendship with Bryant was based on a love for American nature. It was celebrated by another American artist, Asher B. Durand, in a painting called *Kindred Spirits*. In it the painter, holding his palette, and the poet stand together looking at the natural scenery of the Catskill Mountains of New York. As in Cole's paintings, Durand celebrates the native American scene. Cole painted so many landscapes that he became known as the

The Transcendentalists

In 1836 Ralph Waldo Emerson, Margaret Fuller, Bronson Alcott and Henry David Thoreau formed the Transcendental Club in Boston. The transcendentalists celebrated the beauty of nature and the individual. They published a magazine, called *The Dial*. Some of them tried living together at Brook Farm in Massachusetts during the 1840s. Thoreau's book *Walden or Life in the Woods*, published in 1854, was an account of his experiment of living by himself, simply and in harmony with nature. ■

An Early Collector

The wealthy New York merchant Luman Reed (1785–1836) used the profits from his dry goods store to buy art and form one of the most important art collections in the United States. In the early 1830s, Reed began to buy American paintings to encourage and support local artists. When he built a new house in lower Manhattan in 1832, he included a two-room gallery. He asked Thomas Cole, Asher B. Durand and George W. Flagg to decorate the doors to the gallery, which were opened to the public once a week. After he died, a group of his friends purchased his collection and founded the New-York Gallery of the Fine Arts. In 1858, it was given to The New-York Historical Society where the Luman Reed Collection is located today. ■

▲ *This oil on canvas painting of 1836,* The Course of the Empire-Desolation, *is one of a series of five by Thomas Cole. Together the paintings form an allegory or lesson about the rise and fall of a once great country.*

The New York collector, Luman Reed, has been credited with making "native art the fashion" through his support of a number of American artists of his time, including Asher B. Durand, who painted his portrait in oil on canvas in 1835. ▼

founder of the Hudson River School of landscape painting.

Cole began painting in 1825. He often liked to paint groups of pictures built around a theme. Although they were mainly landscapes, these paintings are called allegories because they were intended to teach the viewer a lesson. One such series, *The Course of Empire*, was paid for by the New York collector Luman Reed. It included five paintings that traced the history of an imaginary empire from an untamed wilderness state, like much of the western United States, to ruins, like those Cole had seen in Europe. The idea for it came to Cole while he was in Europe between 1829 and 1832. In Rome he saw the remains of a once great empire. He did not want America to suffer the same fate. Together the paintings in this series are a visual warning to Americans not to take their wealth of natural resources, political freedom and power for granted.

The first landscapes in America were not as grand as Thomas Cole's. They were simple representations of the way the land looked. Later, landscape views served as decorations on mantlepieces and backgrounds for portraits. America was a country without any evidence of the progress of western civilization, and many people regarded it as a sort of Garden of Eden. So, they became interested in what the country looked like. Paintings of natural wonders like Niagara Falls and historical sites such as George Washington's home at Mount Vernon became popular. Sometimes, paintings of historical

▲ *Albert Bierstadt's reputation was based on large paintings of the American West like his oil on canvas* Storm in the Rocky Mountains, Mt. Rosalie *of 1866. To promote these panoramic views of America, Bierstadt not only had prints made of his paintings but he exhibited them around the country and in Europe.*

Traveling Picture Shows

In an age without television or films touring exhibitions of large pictures became a form of entertainment for nineteenth-century viewers. They also became a business for artists like Albert Bierstadt. He himself promoted some of his great pictures by exhibiting them in dramatic, theatrical presentations. Often the room was artificially lit and potted plants enhanced the feeling of being out of doors. These special exhibitions used advertising, press coverage, prints of the painting and paid admission to make a profit for the artist. One of Bierstadt's exhibitions even attracted the attention of British Queen Victoria. ■

sites outside the United States were made by American artists. John Vanderlyn (1775–1852) went to Paris to study in 1796. Inspired by Versailles, he painted a panorama, *The Palace and Garden of Versailles*. A panorama is a wide, overall view of a scene that shows more than the eye would normally see. It was an idea that was introduced into France by the American inventor and painter Robert Fulton. Although Vanderlyn's panorama of Versailles was not very successful when he displayed it in New York, panoramic views remained popular in America in the nineteenth century.

Another mid-nineteenth century painter who glorified America by presenting panoramic views of untamed natural sites was Albert Bierstadt (1830–1902). His scenes of the American West included the Rocky Mountains, the Sierra Nevada and Yosemite. Bierstadt himself promoted these large landscapes by touring them around the country and by making prints based on his paintings. For Bierstadt, his "great pictures" were visual statements of America's "Manifest Destiny," the belief in expanding the country from the Atlantic to the Pacific Oceans.

Large paintings of the wilderness were not the only kind of landscape painting in America in the middle of the nineteenth century.

▲ *John F. Kensett, a Luminist, painted this quiet scene in oil on canvas,* Paradise Rocks, Newport, *about 1865.*

An Internationally Known Painter

Robert Scott Duncanson was born in Seneca County, New York, the son of a Scots-Canadian father and an African-American mother. He moved to Canada and then Cincinnati, Ohio, around 1841. He was influenced by Thomas Cole's landscapes, although he was mostly self-taught. His first visit to Europe in 1852 was made with the help of money from the Anti-Slavery League. Duncanson visited Europe three times and met Alfred Lord Tennyson (1809–92), whose writing inspired some of his paintings. He is the first African-American artist to have established an international reputation. ■

▲ *When Robert Scott Duncanson painted* Landscape with Rainbow *in 1859, the country was on the verge of the Civil War. The rainbow seems to be a beacon of hope for those who sought freedom for black Americans.*

Some artists who are now called Luminists painted quiet scenes of the coast or bodies of water. John F. Kensett, Sanford R. Gifford, Martin Heade and Fitz Hugh Lane were some of these artists. Their paintings showed an interest in light and air. They seem very still and invite the viewer to think about the beauty of the world reflected in them.

For some artists, the beauty to be found in nature sometimes seems to have another meaning. Frederic Edwin Church (1826–1900), one of Thomas Cole's students, painted great, large-scale paintings like his chief rival, Albert Bierstadt. Church's *Twilight in the Wilderness* was

▲ *The 1855 watercolor,* The Lackawanna Valley *is a study for a larger painting. Commissioned by the president of the Delaware and Lackawanna Railroad Company, the company was not satisfied with the finished work. The artist George Inness was only paid seventy-five dollars.*

painted just before the Civil War. It suggests not only the end of the western frontier in America but also the end of America's innocence as a new nation. For Robert Scott Duncanson (approx. 1821–72), nature seemed to promise a new beginning. In his painting, *Landscape with Rainbow*, the rays are like symbols of hope. Duncanson, like his fellow African-Americans, wanted freedom, equality and the end of the national disunity caused by slavery.

Over the years, the dramatic, grand images of the land that Church and Bierstadt painted were gradually replaced by scenes that show the human role in shaping the world. George Inness's (1825–94) painting, *The Lackawanna Valley*, was commissioned by the president of the Delaware, Lackawanna and Western Railroad as an advertisement for the company's Pennsylvania line. Evidence like tree stumps, smokestacks and buildings tell viewers of the increasing industrialization and settlement of America.

7 Pictures of History

▲ *Benjamin West's 1770 choice to use contemporary costume in this oil on canvas,* The Death of General Wolfe, *made this the first composition to depict an event from modern life in the military dress of the day.*

Benjamin West gained his fame as a history painter in England. This is his self-portrait of about 1770. ▼

History painting, which includes the story of real, legendary or biblical heroes as well as actual events, was considered the highest form of painting in Europe. European civilization gave artists many subjects for this kind of art. Usually, these pictures were large and the figures were often posed dramatically and clothed in classical dress. American artists gradually became familiar with this tradition through prints and by traveling abroad. They too wanted to try painting historical pictures. However, as a new nation, the United States had few people and events to commemorate.

One of the first important history paintings produced by an American artist was Benjamin West's *The Death of General Wolfe.* The 1770 painting shows an event from the French and Indian War. In the struggle between the British and the French for the control of the North American interior, the British General James Wolfe (1727–59) suffered a fatal wound. He is shown dying on the battlefield, with concerned comrades around him. He wears the brilliant red coat that gave the English soldiers their nickname, rather than the classical costume of a Roman soldier which people would have expected to see in a history painting at this time. The American Indian looking on reminds the viewer that the scene is not taking place in Europe. The details from real life helped create a more truthful scene than most history paintings depicted. The president of

▲ *This is John Singleton Copley's* Watson and the Shark *painted in oil on canvas in 1778. This painting was so well received that Copley made a copy of it and kept that version for his own collection.*

Watson's Adventure

Although he is best known for his outstanding portraits, John Singleton Copley also produced history paintings. A master of detail, history painting was a natural progression in the work of this talented artist. His most famous history painting is *Watson and the Shark*. Copley was commissioned by Brook Watson, the main character in the picture, to paint this gruesome scene in 1778. Watson was attacked by a shark while swimming in Havana Harbor in Cuba in 1749 and rescued. The shark injured one leg and then bit off Watson's foot. Copley used all his skill and a Romantic style to recreate the dramatic incident. By carefully structuring his composition, Copley draws the audience into this exciting rescue scene. The great shark in the foreground becomes a frightening symbol of evil. Brook Watson commissioned this painting so "that it might serve a most useful Lesson to Youth." For despite his wooden leg, Watson became a successful businessman, a member of the British Parliament and eventually Lord Mayor of London. ■

the Royal Academy, Sir Joshua Reynolds, said "He has treated his subject as it ought to be treated." *The Death of General Wolfe* was a pre-Revolutionary War painting that created its own revolution in the way that artists depicted historical subjects. Benjamin West, who worked in England, was appointed historical painter to King George III the following year. Later, he served as the second president of the Royal Academy. His accomplishments have earned him the title "father of American painting."

Another early American artist who specialized in history paintings was John Trumbull (1756–1843) who came from a prominent Connecticut family. He was the first artist in America to be college educated. During his student days at Harvard, he was most impressed by the work of John Singleton Copley whom he visited in his nearby Boston studio. He joined the Continental Army formed by the American colonies in 1775, witnessed the battle of Bunker Hill and served briefly on George Washington's staff. This helped to earn him a commission as a colonel. He kept both the title and the contacts earned during the Revolutionary War and they served his career well.

Like Copley before him, Trumbull also went to England in the 1780s, where he met and studied with Benjamin West. With his encouragement, and the approval of Thomas Jefferson and John Adams, who even made suggestions for his painting of *The Declaration of Independence*, Trumbull began a national history series. The twelve paintings that he planned were to depict the most important events of the American Revolution. Upon his return to America, he went to great effort to ensure the accuracy of the

▲ *John Trumbull's painting of the signing of* The Declaration of Independence in Congress at the Independence Hall, Philadelphia, July 4th, 1776 *exists in several versions painted between 1786 and 1819.*

Samuel F. B. Morse ▶ *like many artists was interested in painting pictures of historical scenes or events because history paintings such as his oil on canvas* Old House of Representatives *from 1822 were the most respected.*

Samuel F. B. Morse, an Artist and Inventor

Samuel F. B. Morse (1791–1872) is remembered as the inventor of the telegraph and the Morse code. Few people realize that his first choice of a career was to be an artist. In 1811, he went to England with Washington Allston, intending to become a history painter. When he returned to America four years later, he found that the only way he could survive as an artist was to paint portraits. He was one of the founders of the National Academy of Design in New York City and twice served as its president. He also taught painting and sculpture at New York University. Disappointed that he was not asked to paint one of the panels for the Rotunda of the Capitol, he finally gave up the profession of painting in 1836 in favor of a career in science. ■

paintings. In 1817, Congress passed a joint resolution authorizing Trumbull to paint four murals for the new Capitol building: *Declaration of Independence, Resignation of General Washington, Surrender of Lord Cornwallis at Yorktown* and *Surrender of General Burgoyne at Saratoga*. In addition to Trumbull's four paintings, four other paintings about the nation's history were commissioned: John

▲ *This 1861 oil on canvas,* Westward the Course of Empire Takes Its Way *by Emanuel Leutze reflects the belief that the future of America depended on expansion to the west or Manifest Destiny.*

Mutiny on *La Amistad*

Nathaniel Jocelyn (1796-1881), a Connecticut painter and engraver, was inspired by a famous incident that took place in 1839. Thirty-five men and women were captured in Africa and transported to Cuba where they were sold as slaves. As they were being transported to Puerto Rico on the ship *La Amistad*, one of the slaves, Cinque, the subject of Jocelyn's painting, led a rebellion and demanded that the ship return to Africa. The Spanish crew changed course and brought the boat into port at Long Island. The Africans were arrested and the crew freed. However, abolitionists worked for two years to free the Africans. Finally in 1841 the U.S. Supreme Court ruled that the Africans had been taken from their country illegally. ■

Nathaniel Jocelyn painted the noble figure of Cinque in oil on canvas in 1839. He carries a sugar cane stalk, a symbol of the slave labor into which he and his companions were to be sold. ▼

▲ *Emanuel Leutze's oil on canvas painting of a heroic* Washington Crossing the Delaware *on Christmas night in 1776 was actually painted in Germany. It became famous when it was unveiled in 1851. Because of its popularity several versions of the painting were made.*

Vanderlyn's (1775–1852) *Landing of Columbus,* Robert Weir's (1803–89) *Embarkation of the Pilgrims,* John Chapman's (1808–89) *Baptism of Pocahontas* and William Henry Powell's (1823–79) *Discovery of the Mississippi by De Soto, A.D. 1541.* Together these eight large paintings line the walls of the Capitol Rotunda.

The first American to achieve fame both in Europe and America as a history painter was Washington Allston. Educated at Harvard, Allston went to Europe in 1811. His style of painting was called Romantic. It depends on the imagination and an emotional response from the viewer, much like the poetry of his friend, the English poet, Samuel Taylor Coleridge. Coleridge called Allston "a man of genius," as did Charles Dickens, and the best painter yet produced by America." Allston was accompanied to Europe by Samuel F. B. Morse. Morse, better known as an inventor, began his career as a painter. His painting, *The Gallery of the Louvre,* recorded the contents of one gallery in the famous French museum as it appeared to visitors of the time.

Perhaps the most famous American history painting is Emanuel Leutze's (1816–68) *Washington Crossing the Delaware.* The scene shows General Washington heroically leading his soldiers across the Delaware River on Christmas in 1776. The Continental Army surprised the Hessians who were camped in Trenton and won the battle. The picture was originally painted in Germany, but when it was shown in New York, it was so popular that over fifty thousand people paid to see it. In it, Washington's example of courage seems to assure viewers that goodness and virtue will succeed, a message that is found in many history paintings.

31

8 Carved and Modeled Sculpture

▲ *A New England stone cutter carved this abstract portrait of Mary Harvey of Deerfield, Massachusetts and her child. Mary died giving birth to the child, who did not survive, on December 20, 1785. This image was made for their tombstone.*

Help from Italian Craftsmen

Many American sculptors, including some women, went to Italy in the mid-nineteenth century so that they could make sculpture from the prized Carrara marble. The actual carving was often done by skilled Italian craftsmen. The artist would obtain a block of marble somewhat larger than the final work envisioned and work up the composition in a small clay or plaster version. The small model would be made into an enlarged plaster model that the Italian craftsmen could use as a guide for the finished piece. With the assistance of a machine that helped transfer the proportions, the craftsmen created the final version of the artist's original concept in mable. Much of the actual work was done by these craftsmen. They were talented but they worked for very low wages. It required the genius of the artists themselves, however, to conceive the ideas for these works of art. ■

The petroglyphs that the American Indians left on cave walls are examples of relief carving, the first kind of sculpture created in America. Stone carving is also found in other places that most people do not associate with art—cemeteries. Relief images carved on tombstones by European settlers often attempted to remind people of death and the afterlife by carving angels or skulls and crossbones into the stone. Sometimes the sculptor attempted to create a portrait of the person who had died.

Sculpture in the United States also arose from the practical needs of the people. Signs for shops, figureheads for ships, eagles to symbolize the new nation and various other types of trademarks were early examples of American sculpture. William Rush (1756–1833), a master woodcarver from Philadelphia, is considered America's first important sculptor. His work ranged from the figures of *Comedy and Tragedy* for the Chestnut Street Theater and portrait busts of individuals to anatomical models used in the University of Pennsylvania's Medical School. Rush is pictured carving his allegorical figure of the Schuylkill River in an 1877 painting by another Philadelphia artist, Thomas

Thomas Eakins paid tribute to America's first important sculptor in this imaginary scene, William Rush Carving His Allegorical Figure of the Schuylkill River, *in oil on canvas (1877). The female model was accompanied to the studio by her chaperone, who sits nearby.* ▼

An Unpopular Statue _

Images of George Washington, the first American president and great military leader were usually very popular in America. However Horatio Greenough's large, Neo-Classical sculpture of the first president was very unpopular. Americans did not like to see their first president presented partially nude and seated like a Greek god. Although it was originally placed in the Capitol Rotunda, it was later moved outside and then placed in basement storage in the Smithsonian Institution. Today it is once again on view in the Smithsonian's Museum of History and Technology. There the many interesting details can be carefully studied. Two small figures, on the back of the figure's chair, represent Columbus and an American Indian, symbols for the old and new worlds. ■

◀ *This marble statue of* George Washington *by Horatio Greenough was the first commission given by Congress to an American sculptor. It dates from 1840 but was so unpopular that it spent many years in storage.*

◀ *Hiram Power's* Greek Slave *was called "American art's first antislavery document in marble." It was created in 1851, when slavery was being debated in the United States.*

Eakins (1844–1916). Many people thought that Rush would have become better known if he had been able to work in marble, instead of wood, like European sculptors.

During the first half of the nineteenth century, sculpture was often made in the Neo-Classical style. It is called Neo-Classical because its material and subject matter recall the kind of sculpture that was made in ancient or classical Greece and Rome. In 1825, Horatio Greenough (1805–52) left the United States for Italy where the pure white, Italian, Carrara marble could be easily obtained, so that he could learn how to carve marble. His example attracted other American expatriate sculptors to Italy. Although many artists were able to carve the stone themselves, some hired Italian craftsmen to do the job for them. One example was Greenough's Neo-Classical seated heroic statue of *George Washington.*

It was not until mid-century that American sculptors began to work regularly in marble. Hiram Powers (1805–73) was another American sculptor who worked in Italy. His most famous piece, the *Greek Slave,* 1843, was sent on tour throughout the United States. It became a symbol of democracy as the controversy about slavery was growing, which added to the statue's fame. It grew so popular that it was exhibited in London in 1851 at the Crystal Palace exhibition.

Many American women sculptors also went to work abroad in marble. One group gathered in Italy, and in Rome, they often met at the home of the actress, Charlotte Cushman (1816–76). Sculptors like Harriet Hosmer (1830–1908) modeled their ideas in clay and then left the carving of their works to the expert Italian craftsmen they hired. Hosmer's work often focused on the struggles of women with men and institutions although she is best remembered for her popular statue *Puck*.

The sculptor, John Rogers (1829–1904), who only studied abroad briefly, understood what Americans wanted. He met their needs by creating small pieces showing scenes from everyday American life. Cast in

Small, table top sculptures like The Slave Auction *of 1859 by John Rogers, made in plaster, were very popular with middle-class Americans. Rogers created pieces with many different themes from everyday life. They were sometimes purchased through catalogs and were to be found in many homes.*

▲ *Harriet Hosmer produced this sculpture entitled* Zenobia in Chains *in 1859 in Italy where she worked with Italian carvers. Zenobia, Queen of Palmyra, was captured by the Romans before they destroyed the city in 273 A.D. Hosmer's marble figure is full of grace, nobility and acceptance of her fate. The statue was exhibited in 1863 in the U.S. while the country was in the midst of the Civil War. It was seen by the public, during this terrible time in American history, as inspiration for fighting for what they thought was right and resisting defeat in the struggle to abolish slavery.*

The Marble Faun: A Tale of American Art Students in Italy ____

Nathaniel Hawthorne (1804–64), author of *The Scarlet Letter*, spent two years in Italy. In 1860, after returning home, he published a novel set in Rome called *The Marble Faun*. The characters of the novel include a sculptor and two young women art students who had gone to Rome to study, much like the many American artists who went abroad in the mid-nineteenth century. In the novel the characters frequently visit a classical Greek marble sculpture of a faun, a mythological creature that is half man and half goat, and which gives the novel its title. ■

Edmonia Lewis

Edmonia Lewis (approx. 1845-after 1909) was another sculptor who went to Europe to learn how to carve in stone. Born in upstate New York, her mother was a Chippewa Indian and her father an African-American. Lewis, whose Indian name was Wildfire, was raised by her mother's tribe because she became an orphan at age four. She entered the Young Ladies Preparatory Department of Oberlin College at age thirteen through the help of abolitionists and her brothers. She became interested in making sculpture when she met the sculptors Edward Brackett and Anne Whitney in Boston. Through a sale of one of her first pieces of sculpture and help from friends, she raised enough money to travel to Italy in 1865 to learn stonecarving. In Rome Harriet Hosmer and her friends provided a supportive environment for this young sculptor. Some of Lewis's sculptures focused on the American Indian and the struggle of black Americans in the U.S. to free themselves from slavery. ■

▲ General Andrew Jackson, *who became president in 1828 is an early American war hero commemorated in bronze. This equestrian statue of (1848–52) is by Clark Mills (1815–83). The statue was erected in Lafayette Square in Washington, D.C., opposite the White House, for the Jackson Memorial Committee. It was so admired that Mills became the official sculptor to the U.S. Congress.*

hard plaster, these three-dimensional genre scenes were sold by catalog throughout the country. Although most of his pieces were of charming scenes, some did reflect the harsh reality of the period in which they were created, as his sculpture, *The Slave Auction*, did in 1859.

As the Civil War changed the country, so too did it change the type of sculpture that was created. To meet the demand for post-war memorial statues in public places, sculptors began casting their statues in bronze. This durable material allowed the sculptures to be placed outdoors, so that many more Americans from all walks of life could see them and be reminded of both famous and little-known heroes and important events that shaped America's history.

Hero of the Common Man

Andrew Jackson (1767–1845) was the first president to come from humble origins. His election as president of the United States in 1828 was seen as a great victory for the common people. He was a popular figure and helped to usher in a new period in American history that is often called Jacksonian Democracy. He began his career as a lawyer but came to the attention of the people at the battle of New Orleans in 1815, at the very end of the War of 1812. His exploits included crushing the Creek Indians who sided with the British during the war. For his actions, he was nicknamed Old Hickory because of his toughness, but later his opponents called him King Andrew and founded the Whig Party in 1834 to oppose him. Although he was seen as the leader of a political movement that expanded democracy, his dictatorial ways caused him to be censured by the U.S. Senate, an action that his supporters were later able to overturn. He retired to his grand home outside Nashville, Tennessee. ■

9 Everyday Life in America

George Caleb Bingham made a ▶
George Caleb Bingham made a ▶
number of paintings with political
themes. The artist was involved in
politics himself and so was very
much aware of the democratic
process he depicted in his 1854 oil
on canvas painting,
The Verdict of the People.
Bingham's political activities
included campaigning for the
election of William Henry Harrison
in 1840. In 1846 Bingham was
elected to the Missouri state
legislature. From 1862 to 1865 he
was State treasurer.

British Interest _____

The first American Museum to be established outside the U.S. is the American Museum in Britain. Located in Bath, England, it was founded in 1959 to teach people about the country's history and arts. Through a series of rooms the museum presents life in America from the late seventeenth to mid-nineteenth centuries. ■

Pictures of ordinary people in scenes from everyday life are called genre paintings. From the 1830s until the beginning of the Civil War, genre pictures were especially popular with Americans. Because they dealt with many different types of people and activities in various parts of the United States, genre paintings had a wide audience. Subjects ranged from parties to politics. Anything that showed life as it was in America was popular. Genre scenes were painted by anonymous artists as well as leading painters. George Caleb Bingham was the first important American artist brought up in the West. Many of his scenes show mid-western life on the river, elections and politicians. Bingham himself was active in politics and expresses that

Quilting Bees _____

In rural America in the 1800s, distances between houses were great. This made social gatherings difficult. Americans often used social events to meet practical needs like making quilts, raising barns or husking corn. The activity was generally followed by supper and dancing. ■

◀ *The artist John Lewis Krimmel was one of many who depicted the quilting bee, in this 1813 oil on canvas entitled* Quilting Frolic.

Independence Day was a favorite subject ▶
for many American artists such as Lilly Martin
Spencer. Martin was perhaps the most popular
female genre painter of the mid-nineteenth
century for her paintings were widely
reproduced as popular prints for the home. In
her oil on canvas, The Artist and Her Family at
a Fourth of July Picnic *(about 1864), the artist*
includes portraits of herself and her family.

Jonathan Fisher painted Late Harvest *in oil on*
canvas in 1804 from vegetables and fruit grown
on his farm. Many self-taught painters, like
Fisher and women artists were often limited to
making still life paintings of objects found in
their homes. ▼

interest in *The Verdict of the People* of about 1854.

Few political scenes include women in the midst of the activities. However in settings of celebration, like Lilly Martin Spencer's (1822–1902) *The Artist and Her Family at a Fourth of July Picnic*, women are included as part of the community. Women artists like Spencer, who was born in England, were often restricted in what they could paint. They were not allowed to join life-drawing classes where nudes were studied. Often they were limited to making still life paintings of humble objects such as fruit and flowers.

Interest in art in America increased during the early nineteenth century. To meet the new demand for visual images, Nathaniel Currier (1813–88) and J. Merritt Ives (1824–95) published prints that covered almost every aspect of life in America. Lithographs by Currier

Smithsonian Institution: A Mirror of American Life_____

Although the Smithsonian Institution is often thought of as America's museum, it was actually established with funds received from a bequest by a British scientist, James Smithson (1765–1829). Established by an Act of Congress in 1846, it was intended to be "an establishment for the increase and diffusion of knowledge." That same year, the architect, James Renwick (1818–95) began the design for the Castle, the turreted building that is now the Smithsonian's administrative headquarters in Washington, D.C.

The Smithsonian Institution is the largest museum complex in the world. It is sometimes called the nation's attic because of the great variety of objects it has collected in its 150 year history. They are housed in many different museums and bureaus, including the Museum of the American Indian, the Cooper-Hewitt National Museum of Design and the Archives of American Art, a research center and microfilm library, which are all located in New York City. ■

and Ives covered a wide variety of subjects: holidays, sports, western scenes, religious subjects, current events and the Spanish communities in the southwest were all represented. Currier and Ives prints made it possible for even middle-class families to buy and enjoy art. Today, their lithographs are still used on greeting cards and calendars.

Prints were also the means by which an earlier artist, John James Audubon (1785–1851) recorded the birds and animals usually found in Pennsylvania and the Ohio Valley. Audubon took his work to London in 1826. After his drawings were published as prints, Audubon became famous throughout America and elsewhere for his careful depictions of American nature.

As more people became interested in art, many wanted to create it

▲ *John James Audubon is remembered for his many renderings of birds of North America, like this print,* Snowy Egret.

▲ *This is a detail from a popular Currier and Ives print,* Central Park, Winter, The Skating Pond, *produced in 1862.*

Cornelius Krieghoff's The Habitant Farm *painted in oil on canvas in 1856 is full of the details of Canadian country life.* ▼

A Canadian Painter of Everyday Life

The paintings of Cornelius Krieghoff (1815–72) recall everyday life in Canada in the mid-nineteenth century as Currier and Ives's prints do in the United States. Paintings entitled *The Blacksmith Shop, After the Ball* and his masterpiece *Merry-making* of 1860 are filled with details of daily life. Krieghoff was born in Amsterdam and may have trained as a painter in Düsseldorf. He eventually moved to Toronto and exhibited with the Toronto Society of Arts in 1847. In 1848, he tried his hand at printmaking, publishing a set of four lithographs, *Illustrative of Life in Lower Canada*, and later planned a "panorama of Canada" for popular entertainment. However, it is for his snow scenes and genre compositions that he is now remembered. ■

Eastman Johnson's 1859 painting in oil on ▶ canvas was originally called Negro Life in the South. *The name was later changed to* Old Kentucky Home, *the title of Stephen Foster's popular song of 1853. The painting was exhibited in 1859 and was an instant success. Johnson used his father's servants and house in Washington, D.C. as models for this detailed domestic scene.*

The Gift to Be Simple

The Shakers, a Christian community related to the Quakers, took their name from the shaking, dance-like movements displayed during their religious meetings. The first seven Shakers came to America in 1774 from Manchester, England. By the mid-nineteenth century, there were over 6,000 members and eighteen communal settlements. The principles of order, harmony and usefulness guided their lives and were applied to everything that they made. ■

The simple life style of the Shakers and their excellent woodworking technique is reflected in this nineteenth century room of a young child. ▼

themselves. Some, like the Quaker Edward Hicks (1780–1849) worked at jobs related to the fine arts. Hicks was a sign and carriage painter who lived in Pennsylvania. He made more than one hundred versions of his most famous painting, *The Peaceable Kingdom*. Painters like Hicks who did not go to art school or were not trained by other professional artists are called folk artists. Folk artists spend much time designing and decorating objects useful in everyday life such as weather vanes, bird decoys for hunting, quilts, and many other things. This work by untrained artists, whose names are often no longer known and which tells us much about life in America is called Folk Art. For example, the smooth, clean lines of many of the objects made by members of the religious group known as the Shakers reflect their plain and simple life style.

The plain and simple life that characterized America during the first half of the nineteenth century was also captured by trained professionals such as William Sidney Mount (1807–68). Mount was a great observer of people. He recorded the smallest details of human behavior in his paintings. In *The Power of Music* of 1847, Mount tackled the issue of racial inequality in his touching observation of a young black boy excluded from the merrymaking recorded in the painting. Another painter of note, Eastman Johnson (1824-1906), recorded the daily life of slaves in his 1859 painting *Old Kentucky Home*. At first glance Johnson seems to paint a picture that defenders of slavery wanted the world to believe: people living a simple life under conditions of slavery were well-fed, comfortable and happy. However, a closer look at Johnson's painting reveals that the black people live in squalor in the shadow of a white man's splendid home at the right in the painting. As the nineteenth century unfolded, political events increasingly became subjects for American artists.

10 The Civil War and Reconstruction

▲ Forever Free *produced by Edmonia Lewis in marble in Rome in 1867 captured the reaction to Abraham Lincoln's words that all slaves "...are, and henceforward shall be, free."*

The Freedmen's Bureau

Reconstruction, the period following the Civil War, was helped along by a program set up by the Department of War in 1865. The Freedmen's Bureau supplied medical and legal aid as well as food to newly freed blacks and needy whites. Several schools and educational institutions were also established. Officials of the Freedmen's Bureau helped organize the Union Leagues, which were societies pledged to support the government. ■

The Civil War in America created a divided nation. It also gave artists ideas and opportunities to create paintings and sculptures for years after the conflict was settled. African-American artists like Edmonia Lewis, discussed in chapter eight, was one such artist. Her work, *Forever Free*, of 1867 was one of the earliest sculptures to address the issues of slavery and freedom.

Another African-American artist George Mitchell Bannister (approx. 1826–1901), participated in the anti-slavery activities in Boston during the Civil War. Born in Canada, he was dedicated to the idea of harmony in human relations as well as in art.

Photography was introduced to America in the late 1830s by Samuel F.B. Morse, after a visit to Paris. By the time of the Civil War,

Reconstruction Observed

Georges Clemenceau (1841–1929), who was to become Prime Minister of France, arrived in the U.S. in 1865. Clemenceau wrote: "Everywhere you look, you notice political or social problems. But in the United States there is fortunately a strange ability to bend with the wind, to recognize and profit from mistakes...." ■

▲ *Alexander Gardner (1821–82) worked for the photographer Matthew Brady before starting his own studio. His photographs, like* Union Burial Detail at Work After the Battle of Antietam *(1862) show the reality and horror of death on the battlefield.*

it was possible to use the medium on the battlefields. Matthew Brady (1823–96), perhaps the Civil War's best known photographer, may have studied painting before opening his daguerreotype studios in New York and Washington D.C. after 1844. Brady's grim photographs of Civil War battlefields documented the horror of war as no one had been able to show it previously. His photographic portraits included many political figures. Abraham Lincoln is said to have given some of the credit for his success in the presidential election of 1860 to Brady's portrait of him.

Winslow Homer (1836–1910) witnessed many different kinds of war-related events during his work as an illustrator during the Civil War. His early paintings as a professional artist drew on many of them. His picture of a former slave owner visiting her newly freed servants, entitled *A Visit from the Old Mistress*, says much about the conditions both blacks and whites found themselves in after the war's end.

In the years following the Civil War, Americans rose to the task of rebuilding their country. During the period of Reconstruction the nation did not forget its Civil War heroes. Many memorials were erected to figures, like Robert Gould Shaw and his men, who distinguished themselves on the field of battle.

▲ *Matthew Brady took this photo of Abraham Lincoln on February 27, 1860 about the time he was selected to be the Republican candidate for president.*

For many southerners, both black and white, emancipation forged new relationships and lifestyles. In Winslow Homer's oil on canvas A Visit from the Old Mistress, *of 1876, a former slave owner looks in on her old servants.* ▼

A Fitting Memorial

Robert Gould Shaw's family was dedicated to the abolition of slavery. They provided money to train African-American soldiers and wanted their son to fight for the Union cause. Shaw was the commander of the first African-American unit to serve in the Civil War. In 1863, he was killed in the battle of Fort Wagner in South Carolina and buried with his men in a mass grave. Joshua Smith, a former servant and fugitive slave, founded the Shaw Memorial Committee, which commissioned Augustus Saint-Gaudens to create a memorial for the Boston Common. ■

11 Centennial Celebrations and the Industrial Era

▲ *Americans celebrated their nation's first hundred years of independence in 1876 with The Centennial Exhibition held in Philadelphia. The Declaration of Independence had been written and signed in this city so it was the perfect place for the celebration. More than 200 exhibitions were mounted in Fairmount Park which can be seen in this 1876 photo. About 10 million people, representing one-fifth of the population of the United States, paid fifty cents each to see the exhibits about American history and culture, art, science, modern inventions and many other themes.*

In the years following the Civil War, Americans had another chance at a fresh start. The industrial revolution that had begun before the Civil War picked up where it had been interrupted. Americans, who had long believed in the idea of progress, moved in great numbers from rural areas to the cities. These changes in the lives of the average American were often reflected at the Centennial Exposition at Philadelphia in 1876. The Exposition was a world's fair organized to celebrate the hundredth anniversary of American independence from Great Britain. The combination of both new and old American art collected together for this exposition made it the largest art exhibition ever held in America. It was also the most popular department of the Exposition. For the first time, Americans could look back at what had been done in American art over the past hundred years. It even gave many artists and architects ideas for new paintings and buildings that seemed to be from the colonial past. So many things that looked back to the past were made that the period following the Centennial Exposition is sometimes called the Colonial Revival. Thomas Eakins's painting of the early American sculptor, *William Rush Carving His Allegorical Figure of the Schuylkill River*, illustrated on page 32, is an example of a Colonial Revival painting.

The old art was very different from the Exposition's most talked about piece, a sculpture called *La Première Pose (The First Pose)* by Howard Roberts (1843–1900). This piece showed a seated nude who was not pretending to be an imaginary figure from literature or history, but simply the artist's model. It marked the end of the popular taste for Neo-Classical sculpture. *The First Pose* was not the only art work to present something in a very realistic way. Thomas Eakins's tribute to the great American doctor, Samuel Gross was also very true to life. It showed the physician explaining a surgical procedure to his students during one of his teaching clinics. It was so convincing that it had to be shown in the Medical Department of the Exposition and not

◀ Study abroad introduced American artists such as Howard Roberts to techniques and methods, such as working from the nude model, that distinguished European art. Roberts's 1873 marble sculpture, La Première Pose (The First Pose) *reflects this new awareness.*

Rebuilding a City

Not all the rebuilding after the Civil War arose from the destruction of the war. Chicago, which the writer, Bret Harte, called "the Queen of the West" suffered major damage after a fire in 1871. One third of the city was destroyed and had to be rebuilt. ◼

On October 8, 1871 fire broke out in a ▶ poor residential area of Chicago. After three days one third of the city had been destroyed by the fire. One eyewitness who watched the fire reported, "...the appearance was that of a vast ocean of flames, sweeping in mile long billows and breakers over the doomed city."
The center of the city, seen in this photo taken a few days after the fire, "ceased to exist," another observer said.

Advances in Medicine_

Dr. Samuel D. Gross (1805–84) was a surgeon who also taught at Jefferson Medical College. At the beginning of the Civil War, it was the largest medical school in America. Dr. Gross was well-known in both America and Europe. Like the artist, Thomas Eakins, he came from Philadelphia. After the Civil War, there were many medical improvements. Thomas Eakins painted a portrait of Dr. Gross that reminded the world that the doctor, the city of Philadelphia and America led the world in modern surgical techniques. ■

Dr. Samuel Gross, the main character in ▶ *this 1875 painting* The Gross Clinic *by Thomas Eakins, was reknowned as a teacher, surgeon, inventor and writer. The painting caused a sensation in Philadelphia because of its blunt realism.*

in Memorial Hall with the fine art exhibition.

At the Centennial, the work of these two artists and many others like them, seemed to introduce a new spirit into American art. Roberts and Eakins had been classmates at the Pennsylvania Academy of Fine Arts. Like many American artists, they left the country after the Civil War to study art abroad. Eakins spent four years in France working with French masters of painting and sculpture. When he returned home, he tried to use what he had learned in France to teach art in America. His ideas, such as learning to draw the figure from a nude model, were not always popular in America, and he was fired from his teaching job. Eakins was also interested in photography. Sometimes, he used photographs to work out his compositions which gave them a very life-like look. Occasionally, he photographed as well as painted portraits of his friends, as

▲ *As photography became popular, artists experimented with it for study purposes. Thomas Eakins took photographs, such as this portrait of* Walt Whitman, *just before his death in 1891. Eakins sometimes looked to photographs as guides for his paintings.*

he did with the great American poet, Walt Whitman (1819–91). Today, the realism that Eakins introduced is considered an especially important contribution to American art.

The Centennial Exposition introduced other foreign influences as well. The pavilion, or building, for the Land of the Rising Sun, built by Japanese craftspeople, gave Americans their first opportunity to look at authentic Japanese architecture. In the remaining twenty-five years of the nineteenth century, Japan became an increasingly important influence in America. People began collecting Japanese vases and many artists used Japanese elements in their pictures. The Centennial Exposition coincided with a new period of industrial growth in the United States. Paintings like Eastman Johnson's *The Old Stagecoach* of 1871 reminded Americans that the old ways of life were changing rapidly.

▲ *The American belief in the notion of progress and capitalism is evident from the choice of figures included in Christian Schussele's 1862 oil on canvas painting,* Men of Progress, American Inventors. *In this imaginary meeting, inventors who helped the progress of America were gathered together for a group portrait under the symbolic portrait of Benjamin Franklin.*

A National Award

Edward Mitchell Bannister, (1828–1901) was the first African-American to receive a national award for his art. In 1876, he won first prize at the Centennial Exposition in Philadelphia for his painting, *Under the Oaks*. He went to the exhibition to see if the report that he had won was true. When he reached the Committee Rooms, he was not allowed in. Bannister shocked the officials by telling them he had painted the winning picture and he was allowed to enter. Bannister's experience is an indication of the lack of stature that black Americans still had following the Civil War. ∎

▲ *This is Edward Bannister's oil on canvas of 1886,* Approaching Storm. *He painted many New England landscape scenes and became one of the area's best known artists. He taught art from his Providence, Rhode Island studio.*

12 Americans at Home and at Work

Samuel Langhorne Clemens (1835–1910), the writer and humorist who used the pen name Mark Twain, spent much of his career poking fun at Americans who didn't seem to know how to behave. After the Civil War, many became so concerned with money and all that it could buy that he called the period the Gilded Age, a term that is still used today. This term was especially used to describe the lifestyles of the most obviously wealthy Americans, such as William K. Vanderbilt (1849–1920). However life for many other less famous Americans was also quite comfortable after the Civil War. William Merritt Chase's (1849–1916) painting, *A Friendly Call* describes a scene familiar to many well-to-do Americans at the time. Influenced by French Impressionism, Chase's picture is a light-filled, airy painting that seems to have been painted on the spot. A scene from everyday life, the painting reminds the viewer that American artists in great numbers had adopted the Impressionist style of painting, usually

▲ A Friendly Call *was painted in oil on canvas by William Merritt Chase in 1895. The artist used his wife, Alice Gerson Chase, as model for the figure in the painting at right. The artist's studio in Southampton, New York is the room in which Chase's figures sit.*

▲ *In 1873 Samuel Langhorne Clemens, pictured here, and newspaper editor Charles Dudley Warner wrote* The Gilded Age. *It exposed the corruption in business and politics in the U.S. after the Civil War. This book and Clemens's 1869 book* The Innocents Abroad, *gave a picture of life in America at the time.*

A Gilded Age Party

Long after the Gilded Age had ended, the name Vanderbilt symbolized American wealth and power. Charles M. Kurtz (1855–1909) who was active in the art world of the time, described a visit to William K. Vanderbilt's mansion for a Christmas party held there in December, 1883:

Last Thursday I attended Mr. Vanderbilt's Art Reception... Mr. V. entirely remodelled his galleries last summer, and although they seemed to have reached the acme of magnificence before, they are far handsomer now....The whole house was thrown open to the guests, who could wander from one room to another as they chose. There was a splendid lunch served in the immense dining room, an excellent orchestra played all evening in a little balcony between the Art Gallery and one side of the central court of the house, and everything was as "unreal" and fairy-tale like as it was possible to make it...there is nothing, I think to compare with it in the world! I have been through nearly all of the Royal Palaces in Europe, and they are really rather commonplace in comparison to this. ■

46

▲ *The wealthiest Americans, such as the Vanderbilts, lived in opulent mansions like The Breakers, their summer "cottage" by the sea in Newport, Rhode Island. It was designed by Richard Morris Hunt in 1893 and did not suffer the same fate as the Fifth Avenue William K. Vanderbilt Mansion in New York City which was demolished in the twentieth century. This is a photo of the lavish interior of The Breakers.*

Painter of Canada's Gilded Age___

As Canada developed, so too did its desire for a record of the people who were important to its modern history. Working in the years between 1889 and 1916, Robert Harris (1849–1919) painted the newly rich and well-educated as well as the politically and socially powerful of Canada. Harris, who came to Canada from his native Wales at the age of seven, was first trained in Boston art schools. In 1877, he studied first in London and then Paris. After his return, he exhibited with the Ontario Society of Artists in Toronto. By 1880, he was nominated as an academician in the new Royal Canadian Academy of Arts. In 1893, he became its president, and received a medal at the World's Columbian Exposition in Chicago. Today, his portraits are remembered for capturing the lifestyle of an elegant era that disappeared after World War I. ∎

after studying abroad. Some, like the artist Theodore Butler (1861–1936), who married Suzanne Hoschedé, the stepdaughter of famous French Impressionist, Claude Monet (1840–1926), stayed permanently. His friend, Theodore Robinson (1852–96) recorded Butler's marriage in his 1892 painting, *The Wedding March*.

Cecilia Beaux (1863–1942), who also studied in Europe during this period, returned home. She began her long and successful career in New York, where she was friendly with Mariana Griswold Van Rensselaer (1851–1934), an important art critic during the Gilded Age, and the artists Augustus Saint-Gaudens and John La Farge (1835–1910). In 1895, she began teaching painting at the Pennsylvania Academy of the

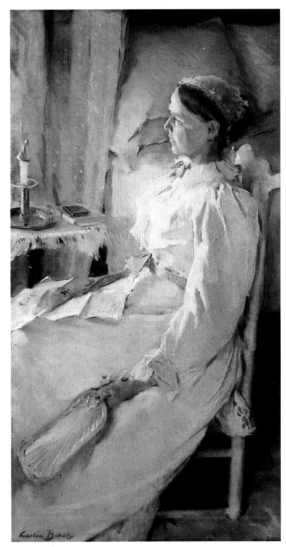

◀ *Cecilia Beaux enjoyed a successful career as a portrait painter of genteel Americans like this oil on canvas portrait of New England Woman (Mrs. Jedediah H. Richards) of 1895. Many wealthy Americans continued to have their portraits painted despite the rising popularity of the camera.*

▲ *Windows like this detail of* Landscape with Peacocks and Peonies *made by the Tiffany Studios were used to decorate many late nineteenth century houses.*

The Art of Stained Glass

In the 1870s, the painters John La Farge (1835–1910) and Louis Comfort Tiffany (1848–1933) began experimenting with stained glass. Artists were becoming increasingly aware of French Impressionism, with its emphasis on light, so a technique like stained glass that depends on light for its dramatic effects was especially fascinating. La Farge invented a new kind of streaky-looking glass that came to be known as opalescent glass because it looked like the surface of the paler-colored variations of opal gemstones. Sometimes it is known as American glass. Tiffany too made much use of the shaded glass. They were making their discoveries when the economic depression that had prevented large domestic projects from being undertaken was coming to an end. As a result, many wealthy Americans began to build or refurbish their homes. Stained glass, fabrics, wallpapers, wood carvings and color design were mixed harmoniously for clients' houses. Stunning stained glass windows featured secular subjects such as landscapes to brighten the homes of privileged Americans during the Gilded Age. ■

Not every American lived in a grand house during the Gilded Age, such as this newly freed family of former slaves painted by Thomas Hovenden in oil on canvas in 1888 entitled Their Pride. *The pride of this American family was not in their material possessions but in the accomplishments of their daughter. By 1888, she and others like her had opportunities to work towards a better life.* ▼

Fine Arts, where she herself had once been a student. She held the position there for twenty years.

The colorful and exciting Impressionist style of painting worked well for scenes of privilege and pleasure. However not all Americans were so fortunate. Some artists, like Thomas Hovenden (1840–95) chose a more realistic view of life. His painting, *Their Pride*, reminds viewers that life for emancipated African-Americans was not as grand as

Realism is a style of painting that ▶
shows things as they are rather than
cleaned up to make a prettier picture. It
was used by artists such as Thomas P.
Anshutz in this oil on canvas painting of
the Ironworkers—Noontime *approx. 1882.*

Labor Unions_____

After the Civil War, workers began to band together and form unions to bargain with the owners of large companies. The American Federation of Labor (A.F.L.) was founded in 1886 and organized workers around a specific job or craft. In 1898, the Erdman Act to help settle disputes between unions and employers through mediation, was passed. ◼

for the average white, middle-class family. However, the softening influence of Impressionism suggests that it was still promising.

The gritty life of a working-class person in the Gilded Age was better suited to realism. Thomas P. Anshutz (1851–1912) was a student of Thomas Eakins at the Pennsylvania Academy of Fine Arts. He used a realistic style to depict steelworkers on their lunch hour in *Ironworkers—Noontime*. Their break for refreshments and relaxation, in the sharp glare of the noonday sun, is different from that of *Woman in Business* by Alice Barber Stephens (1858–1932). A softer way of painting is used to show the details from a scene from daily life familiar to women living in the Gilded Age.

Alice Barber Stephens's 1897 painting in oil ▶
on canvas, Woman in Business *is an interesting*
slice of everyday life from the Gilded Age. An
invention of this period, a department store
provides the backdrop. Shop work and
shopping were two of the "freedoms" post-
Civil War women were allowed.

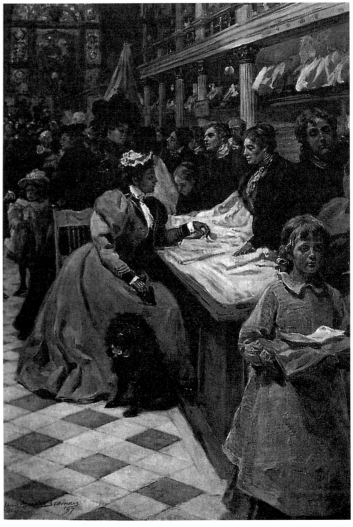

13 American Expatriates and Their World

In 1886, the French Impressionists held their eighth and final group exhibition. Included in that exhibition were seven paintings by an American woman, Mary Cassatt (1844–1926). In that year Americans were also introduced to French Impressionism in an exhibition in New York City. This style of painting was based on broken brushwork, pure color and light. Artists working in this style were thought of as rebels, painters of modern life as seen in the cafes and boulevards of Paris. Mary Cassatt, the daughter of a wealthy family from Pennsylvania, seemed an unlikely member of this group. Yet she was one of many American artists who chose to live abroad after they finished their training as art students.

Americans, particularly those with an interest in art, had traveled to Europe to see the art in museums, purchase some for their collections or be inspired by the scenery before returning home. These late nineteenth-century American expatriates were confident and comfortable enough abroad to live there

The American, Mary Cassatt is usually ▶
associated with the French Impressionists.
However early in her career Spain also
attracted her, as evidenced by her 1873 oil on
canvas Offering the Panale to the Bullfighter.

Americans and Spain

Spain attracted American artists long before they ever went there. Colorful subjects and admiration for the old master painter Diego Velázquez (1599–1660) combined with American history to produce images of Columbus, flamenco dancers, bull fighters, gypsies and guitarists. In 1874, an important collection of Spanish paintings owned by the Duke of Montpensier, who was married to the King of Spain's daughter, was exhibited in Boston to celebrate the new Museum of Fine Arts. Nineteenth-century American painters who visited Spain included Thomas Eakins, Mary Cassatt, John Singer Sargent and William Merritt Chase. ■

An Expatriate Writer _

Some American expatriates were artists. Others, like Henry James (1843–1916), became important writers. He wrote many novels, including *The American, The Europeans,* and *The Portrait of A Lady.* James was very interested in art so some of his novels deal with it. He also wrote much art criticism. Like many other expatriates, he had traveled abroad as a child. He settled in England in 1876 and summed up his decision to live abroad as "my choice, my need, my life." ■

Henry Ossawa Tanner moved to Paris and ▶ *his work was influenced by Impressionism. However, he often drew on themes from the Bible or life in America as he remembered it among his fellow black Americans, as in his oil on canvas of about 1893,* The Banjo Player.

This is Mary Cassatt's portrait of her friend Louisine Elder Havermeyer produced about 1896. ▼

An African-American Expatriate in Paris _____

America's first black expatriate painter was Henry Ossawa Tanner (1859–1937). His ancestors were African, English and American Indian. Like his teacher, Thomas Eakins, Tanner was born in Pennsylvania and studied at the Pennsylvania Academy of Fine Arts. In 1891, he left for Europe and decided to stay in Paris permanently. His work won him fame and he was an active member of the American community of artists in Paris for many years. ■

indefinitely as had American artists before them. Some, like Mary Cassatt, became advisers for other Americans. Her lifelong friend, Louisine Elder Havermeyer (1855–1929), often consulted Cassatt when she bought pieces for her family collection. Much of that collection is now in New York's Metropolitan Museum of Art. Cassatt herself was a collector of the Japanese prints that were readily available

A Scottish Writer Visits America

The Silverado Squatters, 1883, was inspired by the Scots novelist and poet Robert Louis Stevenson's trip to California in 1879 and 1880. During that trip, he married an American woman, Fanny Osbourne (1840–1914). Of John Singer Sargent, who painted his portrait, Stevenson said: "We lost our hearts to him...a person with a kind of exhibition manner and English accent...he gives himself out to be an American." ■

John Singer Sargent painted Robert Louis ▶ Stevenson *in oil on canvas as he appeared in about 1887, less than eight years before his untimely death.*

▲ *William Harnett was a master of fooling the eye into believing a flat canvas held three dimensional objects, as his oil on canvas masterpiece,* After the Hunt *of 1885 attests. He learned the craft of painting in Germany.*

in Paris. They influenced her own work which often used a mother and child theme as subject matter. Her color prints inspired by these Japanese works were a great success.

Another American whose family's lifestyle allowed him to live in Europe was John Singer Sargent (1856–1925). Sargent's upbringing provided him with an introduction to many of the people who later hired him to paint their portraits. He painted in a flashy, Impressionist style that flattered his wealthy sitters and made him one of the most sought after painters of his day. Sargent left Paris in 1885 after one of his portraits received bad reviews. He joined another group of American expatriate artists in Broadway, in Worcestershire, England. Among his paintings are portraits of the writers, Henry James and the Scot Robert Louis Stevenson (1850–94). Other works reflected his travels to places like Venice and the Alps. During a visit to America in 1889 and 1890, Sargent was commissioned to paint a mural for the new Boston Public Library. It was a task that took him thirty years to complete and provided him with many opportunities to visit America.

Most of those who went abroad after the Civil War studied in Paris, where they came under the influence of Impressionism. However some, like William Michael Harnett (1849–92) preferred to go to Germany, which had replaced London as the favored place for art students in the first half of the nineteenth century. German art training enabled artists like Harnett to produce very careful, exact works and Harnett became a master of paintings that were meant to fool the eye. Still-life paintings like *After the Hunt* appeared so real that the viewer almost expected to reach out and be able to touch the various elements of the composition.

Perhaps the most famous American expatriate of all was James McNeill Whistler. Like Cassatt and Sargent, he traveled abroad with his family as a boy. For awhile, they lived in Russia. He studied drawing at the Imperial Academy in St. Petersburg. In 1851, he entered the United States Military Academy at West Point, New York. However, he was dismissed because of his conduct in 1855, and left America never to return. In Paris, he enjoyed living an offbeat lifestyle with other young bohemians.

Whistler became known as much for his wit and appearance as for his art. In 1863, his painting, *The White Girl, No.1*, was rejected for the French Salon along with paintings by other avant-garde artists such as the Impressionists. They exhibited together at a special exhibition that was arranged for all the art rejected by the official Salon. It was called the *Salon des Refusés*. The slightly untidy-looking girl in a white dress in Whistler's painting, against an all white background, did not appeal to most viewers. Shortly after this disappointment, Whistler moved to London.

Whistler's paintings of the 1870s include two that helped to make his reputation. One is the famous portrait of his mother, which he called *Arrangement in Black and Grey, No. 1* because he did not think it mattered who it represented. He thought of it as an exercise in placing colors and shapes together on a piece of canvas. The unusual, unbalanced way that Whistler placed them was influenced by the Japanese prints that were all the rage in Paris. The other painting is a picture of fireworks at night. It is so abstract that the English critic, John Ruskin, accused Whistler of "flinging a pot of paint in the public's face."

▲ *James McNeill Whistler's oil on canvas of fireworks over the Thames River in London, called* Nocturne in Black and Gold: The Falling Rocket, *was considered so abstract when it was painted in 1875, that viewers were insulted by it. It helped push art in the direction of abstraction.*

A Canadian Painter of Modern Life __

Like his American friends, the painters Maurice Prendergast (1859–1924), William Glackens (1870–1938) and Robert Henri (1865–1929), James Wilson Morrice (1865–1924) was interested in scenes of modern life. He met them, and possibly Whistler, in Paris in 1891. From 1901, he exhibited with the International Society of Sculptors, Painters and Gravers in London. Morrice enjoyed being an expatriate, painting cafe life and the French seaside in an avant-garde manner. Although he made his home in Paris, he returned to Canada every winter to paint local scenes. ■

14 Painting Modern Life

Many Americans who went to France for art training came under the influence of the French Impressionists. The Impressionists were interested in painting scenes from modern life using broken brushwork and bright colors. The American public was first introduced to Impressionism through an exhibition held in New York in 1886. This new style of painting received none of the violent criticism its debut inspired in France. As more and more art students went abroad to study, they adopted this colorful style.

After the first treaty between America and Japan was negotiated in 1854, Japanese goods were exported to Europe and America. People were intrigued by the different appearance of Japanese art and artists tried to give their work an oriental look. During the last quarter of the nineteenth century, Japanese objects began to appear in paintings. Some of the more progressive artists used the simpler composition and cut-off perspective that they saw in Japanese prints in France. These paintings of contemporary life were also influenced by the increased use of photography which makes them seem very modern. James McNeill Whistler is probably the best known artist who incorporated Japanese influences in his paintings. Mary Cassatt, Arthur Wesley Dow and John LaFarge, who actually visited Japan in 1886, were just a few artists who looked to Japan for inspiration.

Many of those who returned home began to paint out-of-doors, as they had while abroad. In the last decades of the nineteenth century, sketch clubs and artists' colonies were formed throughout the country. From Shinnecock on Long Island, New York to Provincetown on Cape Cod in Massachusetts, and at many other locations in between, artists gathered

▲ *Frank Benson's (1862–1951) fresh brushwork and the quality of light he captured in* Rainy Day, *painted in oil on canvas, points directly to the influence of the French Impressionists. The way Benson organized the composition of the painting shows the influence of Japanese art. A piece of Japanese pottery sits on the table on the left.*

A Canadian Landscape Painter Abroad

Although Horatio Walker (1858–1938) is remembered as a painter of Canada's farms and peasants, he spent much of his time in the United States and Europe. While visiting Europe in 1882, he was much impressed by the work of the famous French painter, Jean François Millet (1814–75). When he returned to Quebec in 1883, he began painting in a style like the French Barbizon school that Millet represented. His paintings were successfully sold by the Montross Gallery in New York, and so, beginning in 1885, he moved to New York City for the winter season. From 1900 until 1905, he lived in Paris, but despite all of his travels, he returned each year to Canada, where he spent each summer painting. By 1907, he was considered the most famous artist born in Canada and in 1915 became president of the Canadian Art Club. ∎

The Blizzard of '88 ___

In March of 1888 a snowstorm that has become legendary struck parts of the U.S. Some artists were intrigued by the visual effects of the blizzard. The art critic Charles M. Kurtz, described it graphically:

... In the morning the ground was covered to a depth of nearly two feet....All the street cars and elevated railroad trains had stopped running. No ferryboats or railroad trains came to or departed from the city! Every kind of business was stopped. There was a regular "blizzard" on. The wind was terrific and the snow continued to come down fast....They say there are drifts in the Park that completely cover the tall iron fence! Where a path has been shoveled out on 20th Street, the wall of snow is over ten feet high! It comes clear up to the globes on the gas posts. All the electric lights are out; most of the wires are down....Downtown everything is stopped. Many people have been frozen to death; some have been lost in the snow....We have had no mails and no news from the West. ■

▲ *John Twachtman captured the feeling of cold, winter light in his impression of the* View from the Terrace *of about 1890.*

together to paint scenes from everyday life in the open air.

In 1898, the first of the annual exhibitions by a group called The Ten was held in New York. They unofficially formed an American Academy of Impressionism. Included were paintings by Childe Hassam, J. Alden Weir, John Twachtman, Willard Metcalf, Edmund Tarbell, Frank Benson, Joseph DeCamp, Thomas Dewing, Edward Simmons and Robert Reid. Later William Merritt Chase joined the group. They continued to exhibit as a group for twenty years and had a strong influence on the direction that American art took. In addition to being interesting to look at, the paintings of the American Impressionists, reveal much about an era that has long since passed.

Thomas Hovenden went abroad to complete his art training. This oil on canvas of 1890 entitled Breaking Home Ties *depicts a scene familiar to many in the late 1800s, who left home to find their way in the world.* ▼

The March King ___

John Philip Sousa (1854–1932) grew up in Washington, D.C. during the Civil War, and was much influenced by the patriotic feelings that the war stirred in people. He joined the U.S. Marine Band and eventually became its leader for twelve years. He is best known for his distinctly American marches. They stand in sharp contrast to the Impressionist style of music gaining popularity in Europe, with its gentle melodies and delicate sound. When Sousa and his band toured Europe his music was so popular that one British paper called him the "March King", an unofficial title that he still holds. ■

15 The Golden Door

In 1884 Charles Ulrich painted his oil on ▶ canvas In the Land of Promise—Castle Garden. *Castle Garden, originally a fort, was converted in 1855 and, until 1890, was used as a receiving station for the immigrants to America.*

Hull House

Chicago's immigrants were helped by Jane Addams (1860–1935) and Ellen Gates Starr (1859–1940), social workers who tried to improve living conditions for immigrants, women and the poor. They founded Hull House so that people could take courses to help them to learn English and find jobs in their new country. Hull House also had an art studio. ■

Charles Felix Blauvelt painted A German Immigrant Inquiring His Way *in oil on canvas in 1855. The Germans, one of the earlier nationalities to come to America, were quickly assimilated.* ▼

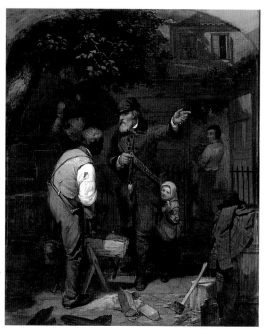

All Americans, except for the American Indians, are fairly recent immigrants, as their ancestors came to the U.S. from other countries. The early immigrants came from Holland, Great Britain and Germany. Beginning life in a new place was never easy, as Robert Weir's (1803–89) *Embarkation of the Pilgrims at Delft Haven, Holland, July 22, 1620* reminds the viewer. About 1883 a new group of people from southern and eastern Europe began coming to the United States in great numbers. These new immigrants were not particularly welcomed by those already in the U.S., nor were the Chinese who began settling in California. Attracted by tales of the good life, they came in ever increasing numbers, believing that the streets of America were paved with gold. As artists began to concern themselves more and more with scenes from everyday life, a few chose these newcomers as the subjects for their pictures.

Charles Felix Blauvelt (1824–1900) chose a German, a member of one of the earlier groups to come to America, for his 1855 painting, *A German Immigrant Inquiring His Way*. However as the century progressed, the newer groups of immigrants were also represented in increasing numbers. The photographer Arnold Genthe (1869–1942), himself a German, began to record the Chinese immigrants who lived in San Francisco's Chinatown. On the east coast, the Italian artist, Joseph Stella (1877–1946), used his own people as models for some of his sketches. The printmaker and writer, Joseph Pennell

▲ *Arnold Genthe photographed these early Chinese immigrants in San Francisco's Chinatown in the late 1800s.*

Liberty Enlightening the World *was a source of inspiration for artists as well as immigrants after its dedication in 1885. In this photo the unfinished statue stands in Paris about 1883.* ▼

(1860–1926), recorded the Federal immigration station which opened in 1892, replacing an earlier one called Castle Garden, to process those arriving on ships as third or steerage class passengers, in his watercolor, *Ellis Island*.

Today, *Liberty Enlightening the World* or The Statue of Liberty as it is more usually called is thought of as a symbol of America's willingness to accept people from other countries. The statue is over 150-feet/45-meters tall. It was designed by the French sculptor, Frédéric Auguste Bartholdi (1834–1904) and was a gift from the French people in memory of the aid they gave to Americans during the War of Independence. It took more than ten years to complete, and was sent to America without a base. The money to build its tall pedestal, designed by Richard Morris Hunt (1827–95) was raised by the American public. One of the fundraising efforts was a special art exhibition called The Pedestal Fund Art Loan Exhibition. It was held in New York's National Academy of Design in December of 1883 and was a great success. It was organized by the American artist, William Merritt Chase, who spent much time traveling abroad. On the base of that pedestal is a poem, "The New Colossus," written by the poet Emma Lazarus (1849–87). It summed up foreigners' hopes for building a new life in America.

> *Give me your tired, your poor,*
> *Your huddled masses yearning to breathe free,*
> *The wretched refuse of your teeming shore.*
> *Send these, the homeless, tempest-tost to me,*
> *I lift my lamp beside the golden door!*

A Warm Welcome

An eyewitness account of the dedication of the Statue of Liberty in New York harbor was given by the American art critic Charles M. Kurtz, on June 21, 1885. *It was a beautiful morning...as I rode down to the battery on the elevated road, to take the steamer....Quite a number of vessels were there before us....The boats formed in procession—about one hundred vessels in line and an almost countless number of tugs, yachts and all kinds of small craft—and we moved towards the city at about eleven o'clock....Every boat was decorated with flags and streamers... and...the French and American colors were preeminent, of course. Nearly every boat, too, had music aboard, and between the strains of the "Marseillaise," "Hail Columbia"...and the booming of the cannon from all the forts along the Narrows and from the numerous French and American War vessels, there was quite a racket.* ■

16 The White City

As the nineteenth century entered its final decade, plans were made for another world's fair. It was held in Chicago in 1893 to commemorate the four hundredth anniversary of Columbus's discovery of America and called the World's Columbian Exposition. A large fountain, called the *Barge of State* was designed by the sculptor, Frederick William MacMonnies (1863–1937), as the centerpiece of the basin in the Court of Honor. The Exposition was nicknamed The White City because its buildings seemed so large and bright. The Women's Building contained murals by two of the country's most noted female artists: Mary Cassatt and Mary Fairchild MacMonnies Low (1858–1946). They were intended to celebrate the contributions of women to civilization.

Advances in transportation were also celebrated in the impressively designed Transportation Building. Trains had replaced stagecoaches, luxury ocean liners were replacing tall sailing

▲ *The sparkling effect of the many white buildings that made up the* World's Columbian Exposition *is conveyed in this 1893 photo of the Court of Honor.*

◀ *Mary Cassatt's 1893 mural,* Modern Woman *for the Women's Pavilion has been lost. It is known today only through photographs taken at the time.*

▲ This is Lorado Taft's Fountain of Time *designed for the World's Columbian Exposition of 1893.*

Closing the West

In July 1893, the historian Frederick Jackson Turner (1861–1932) presented a paper called "The Significance of the Frontier in American History" at a meeting of the American Historical Association held at the World's Columbian Exposition. He said that the vast space of the frontier had allowed America to be a melting pot for newcomers. Settlers banded together for survival without much concern about nationality. Now, homesteading opportunities were over and the frontier had been tamed. The seemingly unlimited promise of western land and the prospect of finding gold in the hills had gone. New immigrants, settling in cities, found it difficult to establish themselves and be accepted. ■

▼ Frederick Remington (1861–1909) was good at showing western action and cowboy scenes. By the time Remington created The Bronco Buster *in 1895, the West was officially closed.*

ships, and captains of industry, like John D. Rockefeller (1839–1937) and William Henry Vanderbilt (1821–85) founded huge corporations based on providing quick transportation at low fares. The Transportation Building, with its spectacular curved, golden doorway, drew much attention to its designers, the Chicago firm of Adler and Sullivan.

The Chicago World's Fair included exhibitions from all over the world. The display of American art showed the world that American artists deserved a place in the history of art. Most of the American art displayed had been produced since the Centenial Exposition of 1876. Painters, sculptors, architects, craftsmen, collectors, politicians and scholars collaborated in a variety of projects ranging from churches and monuments to private homes. This spirit of cooperation between artists and the increasing interest in the arts was first recognized around 1880. By the time of the first planning session for the World's Columbian Exposition, the sculptor Augustus Saint-Gaudens said, "This is the greatest meeting of artists since the fifteenth century!" This period in art history is called the American Renaissance.

Although the largest exhibition in America to date, the World's Columbian Exhibition was by no means the only one since the Centennial in 1876. Regional exhibitions were frequent events in the years between the two fairs. Organizations like the American Art Association organized traveling exhibitions for the encouragement and promotion of American art. They gave Americans who were not able to visit the new east coast museums and galleries an opportunity to view American art and the European works wealthy American collectors had purchased. As more and more of Europe's artistic heritage was being transferred and transformed in America, it became clear that American art was finally coming of age.

Bibliography

Brown, Milton W. *American Art to 1900, Painting, Sculpture Architecture.* New York: Harry N. Abrams, 1977.

Collins, Jim and Glenn B. Opitz. *Women Artists in America, 18th Century to the Present.* Poughkeepsie, N.Y.: Apollo, 1980.

D'Alleva, Anne. *Native American Arts and Cultures.* Arts and Cultures series. Worcester, Mass.: Davis Publications, 1993.

Dewhurst, C. Kurt, Betty MacDowell, and Marsha MacDowell. *Artists in America: Folk Art by American Women.* New York: E.P. Dutton, 1979.

Gerdts, William H. *Art Across America, Regional Painting in America, 1710-1920.* 3 vols. New York: Abbeville, 1990.

Glubok, Shirley. *The Art of America in the Gilded Age.* New York: Macmillan, 1974.

Rubenstein, Charlotte Streifer. *American Women Artists; From Early Indian Times to the Present.* Boston: G.K Hall, 1982.

Smith, Bradley. *The U.S.A.: A History.* New York: Thomas Y. Crowell, 1975.

Sullivan, Charles. *America in Poetry, With Paintings, Drawings, Photographs, and Other Works of Art.* New York: Harry N. Abrams, 1992.

—. *Children of Promise. African-American Literature and Art for Young People.* New York: Harry N. Abrams, 1991.

—. *Here Is My Kingdom: Hispanic-American Literature and Art for Young People.* New York: Harry N. Abrams, 1994.

Taylor, Joshua C. *America As Art.* Washington, D.C.: Smithsonian Institution, 1976.

Acknowledgements

The publisher wishes to thank the Archives of American Art/Smithsonian Institution for permission to quote from The Charles M. Kurtz papers on page 55.

Glossary

abstract art Art that does not represent things realistically.

avant-garde Art or ideas that are experimental and pioneering.

bohemian A person who does not live in the generally accepted manner.

commission To hire an artist to create a work of art.

composition The way an artist arranges the lines, colors, shapes, spaces and elements in a painting, print, piece of sculpture or other work.

curator A person who takes care of the art objects in a collection or selects objects for an exhibition.

daguerreotype An early kind of photograph made using a plate treated with chemicals.

engraving A technique in which an image is scratched into a metal plate or a piece of wood. It can then be used to print many copies of the image.

genre Pictures which represent everyday life.

Impressionism A painting movement that began in France in the 1860s and which was opposed to academic painting. To capture the immediate visual impression of a subject was the main concern of Impressionist artists.

landscape A work of art in which representation of the land is the main subject.

lithography A printing process using a stone or a metal plate specially treated so parts of the surface repel ink.

mural A painting or collage produced directly on a wall, or actually affixed to the wall.

panorama A wide view in all directions.

portrait A painting, drawing, photograph, piece of sculpture or other work of a person, especially of the face.

printing A process that allows an image to be reproduced more than once.

Romanticism A poetic style of painting that is usually associated with the late eighteenth century and early nineteenth century. It often stirs the emotions and deals with far away or literary subjects.

still life Pictures of inanimate objects, usually grouped together, such as fruit, flowers, nuts, vegetables, shells, vases, plates, cups, bottles or fabric.

Photo Credits

The producers of this book have made every effort to contact all holders of coprighted works. All copyright holders whom we have been unable to reach are invited to write to Cynthia Parzych Publishing, Inc. so that full acknowledgement may be given in subsequent editions.

The American Museum in Britain: 19 left
Architect of the United States Capitol, Washington: 15 top left, 29 right
Art Institute of Chicago: 54
The Baltimore Museum of Art: 28 left
Boatman's National Bank, St. Louis, Missouri: 36 top
Bowdoin College Museum of Art, Brunswick, Maine, Bequest of James Bowdoin III: 16 left
The British Museum: 9
The Brooklyn Museum: 26
The Butler Institute of American Art, Youngstown, Ohio: 23 right
Chicago Historical Society: 58 bottom
Corcoran Gallery of Art, Washington, D.C.: 30 top, 56 right
Daughters of the American Revolution, Edward Hand Chapter: 31 right
The Detroit Institute of Arts, Detroit, Michigan: 53
Fine Arts Museum of San Francisco: 52
The Free Library of Philadelphia, The Print and Picture Collection: 42
Hampton University Museum, Hampton, Virginia: 51 right
Howard University Gallery of Art, Washington, D.C.: 40 left
Jefferson Medical College of Thomas Jefferson University, Philadelphia, Pennsylvania: 44 top
Library of Congress: 11 bottom
Munson-Williams-Proctor Institute: 21 right
Museum of Fine Arts, Boston: 14 right, 20 bottom (gift of William Sturgis Bigelow)
National Archives, Washington, D.C.: 17
National Cowboy Hall of Fame, Oklahoma City, Oklahoma: 59 bottom
The National Gallery of Art, Washington, D.C.: 20 top, 29 left, 46 right
National Gallery of Canada: 28 right, 38 bottom right
National Museum of American Art/Smithsonian Institution: 21 (gift of John Gellatly), 27 bottom left, 30 bottom, 41 right, 45 bottom
National Museum of American History/Smithsonian Institution: 33 top
National Museum of Women in the Arts, Washington, D.C.: 37 top
National Portrait Gallery/Smithsonian Institution: 10 top left, 14 top left, 15 bottom left
The Newark Museum: 27 top left, 33 bottom
New Haven Colony Historical Society: 31 left
The New-York Historical Society: 25 top right, 34 right, 39 right
The New York Public Library: 24
North Carolina Museum of Art, Raleigh, North Carolina: 56 left
The Peale Museum: 18 right
Pennsylvania Academy of the Fine Arts: 15 right, 47 right
Peter Newark's American Pictures: 18 left, 35
Philadelphia Museum of Art: 32 right, 43 top, 55 left
Private Collection: 8 left and right, 10 right, 11 top, 13 left, 16 right, 19 right, 23 bottom left, 25 left, 27 right, 32 left, 38 left and top right, 39 left, 40 right, 41 left, 43 bottom, 44 bottom, 45 top, 46 left, 47 left, 48 left, 49 top and bottom, 51 left, 55 right, 57 top and bottom, 58 top, 59 top
Stark Museum of Art, Orange, Texas: 22 bottom, 23 top left
Sterling and Francine Clark Art Institute, Williamstown, Massachusetts: 50
The Taft Museum, Cincinnati, Ohio, bequest of Charles Phelps and Anna Sinton Taft: 52 right
The Union League Club: 48
Wadsworth Atheneum, Hartford, Connecticut: 22 top, 34 left
Warner House, Portsmouth, New Hampshire, 10 bottom left
William A. Farnsworth Library and Art Museum, Rockland, Maine: 37 left
Winterthur Museum: 36 bottom
Worcester Art Museum, Worcester, Massachusetts: cover, 12
Yale University Art Gallery: 13 right

Index

INDEX